ADVISER'S GUIDE TO STUDENT ACTIVITIES

Second Edition

Lyn Fiscus

Leadership
Logistics
supporting positive youth development

Leadership Logistics

11086 Glade Ct., Reston, VA 20191-4715

703-860-2259

info@leadershiplogistics.us

www.leadershiplogistics.us

CONTENTS

CHAPTER 3: MEETING MANAGEMENT

CHAPTER 4: FINANCIAL MANAGEMENT

CHAPTER 5: EVALUATION

CHAPTER 6: RECOGNITION

APPENDICES

ABOUT THE AUTHOR

PREFACE

My first year of teaching was also my first year of advising student activities—of course! Don't all new teachers get saddled with some kind of cocurricular advisory or coaching position? I was the freshman cheerleading coach that first year, and the next year I took on SADD and the pep club. Like most people who become activity advisers, I had received no training on how to be an effective adviser.

Unfortunately, it's usually assumed that educators can step into adviser roles using only the knowledge and experience that prepared them to be teachers. Too often, specific training on how to work with groups in a nonacademic setting is overlooked, and educators who find themselves in the role of adviser to a student activity group have to sink or swim on their own.

That's where this book comes in. I hope that by sharing some of what I have learned about advising student activities over the past three decades I can throw a life preserver of sorts to advisers who are trying desperately not to sink under all the demands placed on them. I have focused on the essentials of advising—things I would have appreciated knowing in my early years as an adviser—so the chapters focus on getting started, projects, meetings, finances, evaluation, and recognition. There's more to advising than this, of course, and for those things I refer you to the resources listed in the appendix, but focusing on these basics will at the very least enable you to keep your head above water.

One other thing that might help is a shift in the way you probably view your role as an activity adviser. In my early days as an adviser, I looked at my work with student organizations as sponsoring events and programs: we planned events, we organized activities, we did things. At first, I considered it my responsibility to make sure that all the events and activities on our schedule went smoothly and successfully. I spent a lot more time *doing* than *advising* in those years. It wasn't until I became student council adviser with its accompanying leadership class that I began to see the larger picture: the cocurricular nature of student activities. I gradually came to realize that my responsibility was to teach student leaders how to plan and carry out events, not do them myself. I shifted from a goal-oriented philosophy of activities—the important thing was to have the event or program—to a process-oriented philosophy—the planning process and the execution of the program became the important elements, not just having the event.

In the end, the fact that you held a dance or a pep rally isn't the most important thing. The process of having student leaders plan the event, pull together the elements needed to make it a success, communicate with everyone involved, resolve conflicts, conduct the event, and evaluate its success—that's where the learning occurs.

Teaching goal setting, project planning, communication skills, conflict resolution, time management, and the host of other skills needed to pull an event or program together isn't an easy task, but it is one that will benefit students for the rest of their lives. And that's why I'm a staunch advocate of student activity programs. Students who participate in this type of learning experience gain confidence and leadership skills that will affect their future every bit as much as what they learn in a classroom. Educators who see things like pep rallies as an intrusion on the education process, or as an extra element that is nice but not absolutely necessary, are not seeing the bigger picture. These types of activities are an integral part of the education process.

I encourage you to see yourself not as the sponsor of events and programs, but as the person who helps student leaders use events and programs to learn and practice leadership skills—in short, the adviser. This subtle shift in thinking can make all the difference in your approach, and will help make your advising experience—if it isn't already—an important element in your mission as an educator.

Sincerely,

Lyn Fiscus

GETTING STARTED

Most educators, at some point in their career, are asked to take on the responsibility of working with a student organization. Some view it as an "extra" duty—something that is tacked onto their already full workload—and they give it the minimum attention necessary. Others—whether because they are already interested in the type of activity, they had a good experience with it themselves in school, or they just like new challenges—take on student activity advising with enthusiasm and thrive with it. Few people assume their advising experience with any advance training. Unfortunately, it's usually assumed that educators can step into adviser roles using only the knowledge and experience that prepared them to be teachers. While that knowledge and experience make a good foundation, working with students in an advising capacity requires different skills and attitudes than classroom teaching.

Adviser Responsibilities

What is expected of a student activity adviser? Each district will have its own expectations—and if you are lucky, these are written in a job description—but in general, the responsibilities of activity advisers can be divided into two areas: program functions and educational functions.

Program Functions

Program functions provide for the smooth operation of the organization. In this area, the activity adviser is expected to:

• Be aware of procedures and regulations affecting the group, including how student activities operate in your district and state

- Be familiar with the constitution and bylaws of the organization with which you work
- Establish yearly goals for the group in accordance with the purpose of the organization
- Work with members to plan and carry out activities to achieve the goals of the organization
- Oversee the work of the organization through the officers and committee chairs
- Assist the group in meeting deadlines and achieving goals
- Attend meetings and planned events of the group
- Hold regular meetings and planning sessions with group officers
- Inform members of resources and opportunities that will advance the goals of the organization
- Employ planning, recordkeeping, resource management, and learning environment management practices to maximize the group's effectiveness
- Serve as a resource on administrative/academic issues and how these relate to the functioning of the group
- Obtain administrative approval for all group-sponsored activities.
- Serve as a liaison to the faculty, administration, student body, and community regarding matters related to the organization

- Schedule and supervise fundraising activities
- Administer the receipt and disbursement of organization funds
- Maintain financial records of the group
- Oversee the recruitment or selection of new members
- Oversee the election/selection of officers and committee chairs
- Work with officers to assist them in understanding and carrying out their duties of office
- Provide for the effective transition of officers from one year to the next
- Develop procedures for keeping records and evaluation files
- Provide supervision to ensure student safety during organization activities
- Act as chaperone to members attending workshops and conferences
- Keep principal and staff apprised of the organization's activities
- Provide information on organization activities to local media to promote positive community relations
- Make decisions guided by educational goals.

Educational Functions

Because the activity program is an integral part of the school's mission, providing opportunities for students to expand on and practice what they have learned in the classroom, activity advisers are also educators. In this area, the activity adviser is expected to:

- Express enthusiasm and interest in the group and its activities
- Enlarge the thinking of the group by introducing new ideas and challenging the group on "the way we've always done things"
- Encourage the involvement of all group members
- Conduct leadership training for officers and members
- Work with student members and officers to develop their leadership skills
- Provide support for students to practice their management and leadership skills
- Act as a facilitator of group discussion by summarizing, clarifying, and teaching facilitation skills to members
- Give assistance, guidance, and praise when appropriate.
- Act as a positive critic of the group. Give feedback on how they are doing.
- Conduct regular evaluations of programs and activities
- Be open minded, looking for new ideas and encouraging the best from students
- Form a positive, role-modeling relationship with the officers and members of the group.

The requirements for activity advisers will vary from district to district, and job descriptions often involve little more than a list of activities for which the person is responsible. Check with your administration to determine if a written description exists for an activity adviser. If not, it's a good idea to draft one so that everyone involved knows what is expected when taking on the responsibility of working with a student organization.

Understanding the Organization

Whether you are eager to take on your responsibilities as an activity adviser or are doing it because you were "volunteered," you can do a number of things to make the advising experience positive. The first step in advising a student group is getting to know the purpose and structure of the organization. A student organization—whether it's student council, National Honor Society, pep club, chess club, or science club—exists for a reason. What is the purpose of the group you are advising?

A good place to look for this information is in the organization's constitution and by-laws. While some organizations do a better job than others of clearly spelling out what they are about in a constitution, every group should have a written document that details what its purpose is, who can be members, how officers are elected, how often meetings are held, what committees exist, and so forth. A constitution is simply a written set of rules for a group.

If your organization doesn't have a constitution—or if the one it does have was written years ago when the group was first started—take the time to create one or update it.

(See page 5.) Advisers who operate without written guidelines for a group sometimes find themselves in difficult positions when they need to discipline members or dismiss officers and students and parents demand to see "where that rule is written."

Understand Policies and Expectations

Another important step to take when advising a student organization is to find out what the school policies are that govern activities. Meet with your principal to find out what his or her expectations are for you and what district guidelines exist regarding activities. At the very least, the district will have regulations regarding the finances of a group (see Chapter Four), but are there other policies regarding meetings, elections, membership recruitment, project approval, and so forth?

Find out what your budget is for the organization and what the source of the funding is. Will you have to raise funds to conduct the activities of the group, or does the district provide funding? What policies exist governing how many and what type of fundraisers your group can conduct?

Review Records

A good way to determine just exactly what you've gotten yourself into is to review the records from the prior year. If you are lucky, the previous adviser will have left files with evaluations and other notes regarding the various activities. If you are like many advisers, however, you will start out with nothing. If that's the case, ask the principal,

assistant principal, activity director, or your colleagues what activities or projects your organization has been typically responsible for. Are you required to do these same projects again or can you start from scratch? Is there a master calendar from the previous year that you can review to get a scope of what is involved?

Meet with Officers

One of the best ways to get to know the organization is to meet with the officers. Schedule a meeting with them during the summer if possible or early in the school year. Find out why they belong to the organization, who the members are, how they became involved (sign-ups, elections, etc.), and what they hope to accomplish. Talk with the officers about what you expect of them as student leaders and ask them what they expect of you as their adviser. Discuss such things as coming to meetings on time, attending all events of your group, asking for help if they need it, and so forth.

As the adviser, be clear about what your expectations for them are. Some advisers have their officers and their parents sign a code of conduct with the expectations clearly written out for them as well as the consequences of not living up to those expectations.

One way to ensure that your officers have a clear understanding of their roles and responsibilities is to provide each with an officer notebook. The notebook should include a job description (see page 11), a calendar for the year, a directory of mem-

Constitution & Bylaws

An organization's constitution should be stated in simple, easily understood language and should include only essential items. Most constitutions follow a generally accepted structure, with major parts called articles. The articles follow a logical sequence and each describes an enduring aspect of the organization. The following articles are typical for school organizations:

Article I: **Name**. Statement of the name of the organization.

Article II: **Purpose**. The general purpose or mission of the group.

Article III: **Powers**. Powers vested in the organization; the right of veto by the principal.

Article IV: **Membership**. Definition of membership for the group; qualifications of membership. Who is eligible for membership? Are there any restrictions? How does one become a member? How are members identified?

Article V: **Officers**. Description of the officer positions; qualifications for office; duties and responsibilities of office; executive committee description, if applicable; terms of office; procedure for removal of officers; procedure for filling vacated offices.

Article VI: **Elections**. Establishment of the time, methods, and procedures for nomination, campaigns, and election of members, officers, and advisers.

Article VII: **Meetings**. Frequency of meetings and provisions for special sessions; number of members necessary for a quorum.

Article VIII: **Committees**. Description of standing committees and provisions for the formation of special committees as the need arises.

Article IX: **Finances**. Description of source of group funds; membership dues, if applicable; budget approval process; limitation on how funds may be spent; procedure for requesting funds.

Article X: **Ratification**. Method and procedure for approval of the constitution.

Article XI: **Amendments**. Provisions for amending the constitution.

Bylaws are rules adopted by a group for its own meetings or affairs. Bylaws usually are items that are subject to change more frequently than items in the constitution. Because of this, the process for changing bylaws should be somewhat easier than amending the constitution. Bylaws typically cover such areas as: the parliamentary authority for meetings, specifications for election speeches and campaigns, balloting procedures, timing of elections, times and locations of meetings, and so forth.

ber information (if available), a copy of the constitution and bylaws (if available), and other pertinent information. Officers can add meeting minutes, committee reports, and other information to the notebook as the year proceeds and it will become a valuable record of the group's activities that can be handed down to their successors.

This initial meeting is a crucial step in beginning to build an officer team. The continuing success of an organization depends in large part on the quality of its leaders. The adviser's job will be much easier if the officers take an active role in leading the activities of the group. Discuss what they would like to accomplish during their term of office. What issues would they like to address? What events would they like to undertake? Consider these questions:

• What are you most looking forward to this year?

• What activities our organization has sponsored in the past are you looking forward to doing again this year?

• What activities are you NOT looking forward to this year? Why?

• What is the one thing you most want to accomplish as an officer this year?

Even if you think all the officers already know each other, it's important to take some time to bond as a team. Lead the officers in some icebreaker or boundary breaker activities that will help them learn a little more about each other and what their aspirations are. Discuss what motivated them to become an officer and what they have enjoyed about being a member of your organization. Some groups have a tradition in which the adviser takes the officers out to dinner or they all meet at a local park to begin planning their term of office. These are ideal times to begin the officer team bonding.

Goal Setting

An important step in planning for a successful year is establishing or reaffirming the reason for the group's existence. As a group, you can accomplish great things and make a difference in your school's culture. Don't let your members aimlessly pick up where the organization left off last year, jumping right in to plan fall activities without thinking about why they are doing them and if they really want to do them. What are the group's goals for the year? These goals will help guide the actions that follow. If the group exists to promote school spirit and provide support to the school's athletes, its activities will be very different from those of a group whose aim is to encourage students to further their knowledge of science and help them win scholarships.

Early in the year—even in summer, if possible—get the members of your organization together to determine five or six broad goals they want to work on that relate to the purpose of the group. The goals should be selected by all the members of your group, not imposed by the adviser or the officers. Setting goals as a group helps everyone understand what the group is all about and helps develop a team spirit. (See SMART Goals.)

To begin, brainstorm possible goals by discussing what the group wants to accomplish. A student council might list improving faculty-student relations, creating a positive school climate, promoting active citizenship, or developing leadership skills of members as goals. Honor Society groups might want to encourage an atmosphere of service, promote the value of good character, recognize outstanding scholarship, or help at-risk students improve their study skills. Encourage everyone to participate and record all ideas, no matter how unrealistic.

Discuss the brainstormed list and narrow it down to five or six important goals that everyone can agree to support, rather than a "laundry list" of goals that will be hard to remember and may or may not get done. You may find that several goals can be combined into a broader category.

Once you've determined your main goals it is important to establish a link between your goals and the projects you undertake. (See Project Planning Overview on page 15.) A technique called carousel brainstorming is a good way to generate project ideas for each goal. To do this, write each goal at the top of a separate sheet of chart paper or butcher paper. Divide your organization's members into as many small groups as you have goals. Give each group a different color marker and one of the sheets of paper. Let each group have 2–3 minutes with each goal sheet to record all the ideas they can think of that will help accomplish the goal. For example, to achieve the goal of promoting

SMART Goals

For a goal to be effective, it should be defined in a clear, precise statement that includes the following components:

Specific — Goals are clear and focus on one thing. For example, a goal of "I want to be the best at everything" is too broad. A more specific goal is: "I want to get to school on time," or "I want to get an A in History."

Measurable — Attainment of the goal is something you can measure or determine if it is accomplished. Can you determine if you get to school on time? If you have an A in History? What if your goal is to be a better student? That one is harder to measure—how will you know if you've become "better"?

Achievable — The goal is realistic and attainable. You could probably lose 10 pounds by next month, but losing it by tomorrow is not realistic.

Responsibility rests with me — Meeting the goal is something that you are responsible for making happen; it doesn't depend on someone else. You can't set a goal for a team you're on to have an undefeated season, because it's up to all the members of the team, not just you.

Timeline — The goal has a target for completion. At what point will you know your goal is achieved? The goal of getting an A in history, for example, has a timeline of whatever the grading period is—quarter, semester, etc.

How to Set Group Goals

Brainstorm for possible goals by discussing what members want to accomplish. Everyone should participate in this discussion. Record all ideas, no matter how outlandish or unrealistic they might sound.

Discuss the list in relation to the strengths and weaknesses of the group—what can you realistically hope to accomplish.

Narrow the list down to about five or six important goals that everyone can agree to support.

Select activities/projects to help achieve the goals. It is important to establish a link between your goals and the projects you undertake—don't do an activity if it doesn't support your goals. Some goals may be accomplished in one project, while others require ongoing efforts.

Plan the calendar. Divide the projects into seasons or semesters—ones that would be appropriate for fall, winter, spring, or first semester, second semester. Select one major project for each month or quarter and several lesser projects. The number of projects will depend on how active your group is and how committed the members are.

school spirit, projects might include pep rallies, spirit weeks, selling spirit wear, organizing buses to away games, and so forth. To promote citizenship, activities might be a voter registration drive, citizen of the month award, participation in an online mock election, and conducting school elections. To promote scholarship, activities might be an academic pep rally, after-school tutoring, or student of the month award.

This is not the time to discuss projects; simply list as many ideas as possible. Rotate the sheets from group to group after each time period until all groups have brainstormed for each goal. Once carousel brainstorming is finished, post the lists so everyone can see them.

Calendar Planning

The next phase is to discuss the brainstormed project lists for each goal and begin to evaluate which ideas are desirable and feasible. Sometimes it is helpful to divide the projects into seasons or semesters—ones that would be appropriate for fall, winter, spring, or first semester, second semester. Select activities that group members would like to take on and begin to plan out the year's calendar. Select one major project for each month or quarter and several lesser projects. (See form on page 17.) The number of projects will depend on how active your group is and how committed the members are. It is impossible to accomplish every project the members listed, so select those that best help you achieve your goals for the year.

Every project should help accomplish a goal, otherwise don't do it!

At this point in the process, someone will likely realize that a favorite annual project—Homecoming dance, for example—is not listed. This provides a good opportunity to engage group members in a discussion of why you have sponsored that activity in the past and to evaluate whether it is something you wish to continue doing. (See "Evaluating School Traditions" in Chapter Five.) If a project you've always done isn't helping you achieve one of your current goals, why sponsor it?

With the example of the Homecoming dance, what does your group think it will accomplish by hosting it? Do you want to provide an opportunity for social interaction? Uphold tradition? Generate spirit? Raise money to fund other activities? Consider other projects as well: What's the point of having noontime activities or a class of the year spirit competition? Why have dances? Why take time to do faculty appreciation? Keep in mind that all projects should have a meaningful connection to group goals and to members of the school.

If group members feel strongly that a particular activity should be sponsored, re-examine the goals you have selected. Do they really reflect what you want to accomplish? Perhaps the goals need to be modified to include the reasons for sponsoring the activity.

Once you plan the activities to support the group's goals, go over the calendar of the year so everyone knows what's ahead. Be clear about what you expect as far as number of activities and time commitment and what the consequences will be if members don't live up to expectations.

As the year proceeds, keep the focus on accomplishing the goals that the group members selected. It's easy to get caught up in planning one event after another, but don't forget to talk about why you are planning them. How will the project help achieve a goal? How can you measure its success? Keeping these questions in mind will help focus your efforts and provide a way to evaluate activities upon their completion.

Consider a Theme

One way to help keep the goals fresh in members' minds is to select a theme for the year that encompasses the general intent of the group. The discussion of possible goals and projects you want to undertake will often reveal a general trend or major emphasis of group members. Perhaps their major concern is how to get more students involved or how to raise school spirit, and the majority of activities you've selected support this idea. Brainstorm a catchy slogan or acronym that summarizes the overall focus and use that as your theme for the year. The theme will be easier to remember than a laundry list of goals—and makes for a better graphic design if you decide to create an organization T-shirt that can be worn by group members on special days.

A few themes that schools have found effective include:

- "Go MAD!" (Make A Difference)
- Time for MAGIC (Making A Greater Individual Commitment)
- Let's SHOUT (Spread Happiness Over Untouched Territory)
- STARS (Students Together Are Reaching Success)
- We're All in this Together
- Lead Out Loud!

Take Care of Details

Check your tentative monthly plan against the school's master calendar to ensure that your projects don't conflict with other major school events. Make any necessary adjustments in timing, then be sure to file all the appropriate paperwork required by your school such as master calendar requests, administrative approval, and so forth. Once the calendar is finalized, make a copy and distribute it to officers and group members so they will be able to plan their schedules accordingly.

Build Support for Your Plan

After you've selected your goals and selected activities to support them, be sure to share your plans with the administration and faculty. Send a letter to the faculty or present your organization's goals for the year at the first faculty meeting and ask for their support in helping you achieve them. Stress all the ways your activities support and extend the curriculum. Some faculty members see activities as an annoying distraction and fail to understand how they support the mission of a school. By letting them know the goals you are working toward and the activities you have planned to accomplish those goals, you will help them appreciate the value of activities as an integral part of the education process. Follow up at the end of the year with a report to let them know what you achieved.

Officer Job Descriptions

To perform the job well, the person responsible for a job must know what it entails. Obligations and responsibilities of officers, members, and committee chairs should be written down, analyzed, and evaluated each year. The job description serves a threefold purpose:

1. It ensures that the person holding the job knows the responsibilities of the job.
2. It provides the basis for evaluating the performance of the person holding the job.
3. It establishes what is important in the organization so that resources can be organized accordingly.

Organizations typically elect people to serve as president, vice president, treasurer, and secretary. The secretarial position often is divided into two positions: recording secretary and corresponding secretary. Other positions that can be elected or appointed may include historian, parliamentarian, and committee chair.

If your organization doesn't currently have a written job description for your officers, it would be a good idea to have the current officers create one based on their duties this year. If there is a job description, one of the tasks officers should complete before leaving office is a review and update of the list of duties to reflect current practice. Typical duties for the major student offices are listed below to serve as a guide as you develop or update your job descriptions.

President

Keeping the delicate balance between leading a student organization and encouraging other officers, members, and interested students to take on leadership responsibilities is the challenge the president faces. He or she must be a dynamic, enthusiastic, hard-working individual who is dedicated to the group's success. In short, the president leads and directs the group in its activities. He or she:

- Helps set the direction and goals of the group
- Works with other officers and the adviser to plan the agenda for each meeting
- Is responsible for the smooth running of group meetings
- Helps carry out the group's objectives
- Serves as the official representative of the group to other organizations
- Supervises the performance of the elected officers
- Coordinates the interviewing, selection, and performance of committee chairpersons and task forces
- Serves as an ex-officio member of all committees
- Serves as a role model for members.

Vice President

The job of the vice president can be very rewarding, but it also can be quite tedious. The role of the vice president is often nebulous and specific duties must be defined with the president. An effective president is eager to help develop the vice presidential position into a creative and productive one, but sometimes the president must be reminded to do that. The vice president:

- Works closely with the president
- Assumes the president's duties if necessary
- Coordinates the work of the committees and typically chairs a major committee
- Works with the president and treasurer in budget and calendar preparation
- Helps the president prepare the meeting agenda
- Works behind the scenes to help iron out conflicts between people
- Serves as chairman of the elections committee, and, as such, supervises all elections related to the organization
- Assumes other responsibilities as assigned by the president.

In some organizations, the vice president is the president-elect and will serve one year as vice president before assuming the office of president the following year.

Recording Secretary

Often, the duties of the recording secretary and corresponding secretary are combined into one position, requiring that the officeholder be especially talented. Here, however, the secretarial duties will be considered as two separate but closely related positions. The duties of the recording secretary are much more comprehensive than simply taking minutes. The recording secretary:

- Prepares and distributes the agenda for business meetings
- Notifies members of upcoming meetings
- Takes attendance at meetings, either verbal or written, and keeps permanent attendance records
- Takes minutes of the proceedings of all meetings, including date and place of meeting, presiding officer, and business conducted
- Prepares and distributes the written minutes, with the president's assistance, in a timely manner
- Maintains a file of original agendas and minutes

Corresponding Secretary

The corresponding and recording secretaries work closely together, one helping the other to ensure the work is done. The corresponding secretary:

- Reports, files, and answers all correspondence
- Maintains the files of the organization, including clippings and relevant documents, and establishes a policy, with the recording secretary, concerning the lending of files
- Maintains contact names, addresses, phone numbers, and e-mail addresses of people with whom the organization regularly works
- Keeps copies of activity calendars and special events
- Writes notes of courtesy, thank you, congratulations, and birthday wishes to members, teachers, administrators, and support staff members
- Produces a membership directory of the group.

Treasurer

The treasurer keeps accurate records of all financial transactions, regulating the flow of money—especially when many people want to spend it. The treasurer:

- Works closely with the president and vice president in preparing a workable year-long calendar and budget
- Oversees expenses and revenues
- Maintains an accurate and detailed financial record of all money collected and spent
- Prepares cost-benefit analyses of various projects and activities (i.e. will the expense of time, money, effort, etc., be worthwhile in terms of its benefits of money, improved image, and so forth) and makes concrete suggestions for saving money and increasing efficiency
- Is familiar with school policies regarding the use of student finances and explains them when necessary
- Authorizes payment vouchers, reviews purchase orders, and gives final approval before invoices are paid
- Deposits money (if school policies allow)
- Makes and interprets monthly financial reports to the membership
- Checks that all contracts entered into are signed by the appropriate school officials
- Acts as co-chairman of the fundraising standing committee.

Historian

The historian is charged with developing a pictorial and written record of the highlights of the year. This job can't be done in a few nights; it must be a yearlong effort. This position can be incorporated into an officer's duties or it can be held by a person whose sole responsibility is this assignment. Typically, the historian:

- Records the activities of the year through video, photos, written reports, clippings, etc.
- Prepares a historical document such as a scrapbook, Web site, slide show, video.

Parliamentarian

Groups that operate under parliamentary procedure often find it helpful to have an officer who is knowledgeable about the proper procedures to follow. The parliamentarian:

- Is familiar with *Robert's Rules of Order*
- Offers procedural opinions only when asked to do so by the chairperson and is subject to the limitations of debate and voting that are applied to all nonmember speakers
- Usually chairs the constitution/bylaws revision committee, if the need arises.

Committee Chairperson

Every committee needs a leader, usually called a chairperson or chair. The chair has the final responsibility for the success of the committee and must work with the members to decide WHAT has to be done, WHO will do it, WHERE it will be done, and WHEN it must be completed. The chair also needs to know and communicate how much authority the committee has. To achieve this, the chair should:

- Have a clear understanding of the goal and authority of the committee
- Communicate that goal to the members of the committee
- Schedule meeting times and places, notify members, and insist on attendance
- Establish an agenda and procedures for the meetings to ensure effective communication
- Appoint a committee secretary and ensure that a written record of each meeting is kept and final reports are produced as needed
- Delegate the work to committee members—appoint or elect a secretary or recorder, a treasurer if needed, and establish sub-committees for specific tasks
- Set deadlines for completion of tasks
- Follow up on progress of specific tasks
- Participate in committee discussions and encourage others to do so
- Be diplomatic: facilitate the group, don't dominate it
- Present reports to the general membership or executive committee, as needed.

Project Planning Overview

What goals have we decided to accomplish this year?

1. _____

2. _____

3. _____

4. _____

5. _____

What projects will achieve these goals?

August

Project: _____ # Goal to which it relates: _____

Project: _____ # Goal to which it relates: _____

September

Project: _____ # Goal to which it relates: _____

Project: _____ # Goal to which it relates: _____

October

Project: _____ # Goal to which it relates: _____

Project: _____ # Goal to which it relates: _____

November

Project: _____ # Goal to which it relates: _____

Project: _____ # Goal to which it relates: _____

December

Project: _____ # Goal to which it relates: _____

Project: _____ # Goal to which it relates: _____

January

Project: _____ # Goal to which it relates: _____

Project: _____ # Goal to which it relates: _____

February

Project: _____ # Goal to which it relates: _____

Project: _____ # Goal to which it relates: _____

March

Project: _____ # Goal to which it relates: _____

Project: _____ # Goal to which it relates: _____

April

Project: _____ # Goal to which it relates: _____

Project: _____ # Goal to which it relates: _____

May

Project: _____ # Goal to which it relates: _____

Project: _____ # Goal to which it relates: _____

June

Project: _____ # Goal to which it relates: _____

Project: _____ # Goal to which it relates: _____

Calendar Planning

August	September	October

November	December	January

February	March	April

May	June	July

Chapter 2

ORGANIZING THE WORK

Once you set your goals and plan your calendar for the year, it's time to organize the projects that will enable you to accomplish your goals. Keep in mind that projects are not goals in and of themselves, merely the methods by which you will accomplish your broader goals.

Backwards Planning

To begin planning any project, it's helpful to employ a technique called backwards planning or, to borrow a phrase from Stephen Covey, "begin with the end in mind." Visualize the event or activity as you want it to be and then determine what it will take to make it happen.

For example, if your group had a goal of promoting positive faculty-student relations, you might plan to host an appreciation lunch for faculty and staff members on an in-service training day. Group members envision a nicely decorated cafeteria where faculty and staff members may sit at tables after going through a buffet line with a variety of delectable food choices. Student leaders serve beverages at the tables and bus tables as staff members finish eating. A PowerPoint presentation of candid photos of teachers and staff members doing their work plays continuously on one wall accompanied by inspirational music. Ask yourself: What will it take to make this happen?

Work backwards from what you envision and break the project down into steps that will enable you to accomplish it. In this example, you have several discrete elements that can be broken out:

Decorations. To achieve the objective of having a nicely decorated cafeteria you must determine what decorations you want and obtain them. If you plan to order them from a catalog, determine how much time is needed to get a purchase order, place the order, and have the decorations shipped to you. Back up from the date of the faculty lunch and set a deadline for ordering the decorations that will ensure they arrive in time. You will also need to recruit and schedule people to help decorate the cafeteria before the lunch.

Food. To achieve the objective of having a variety of delectable food choices you must determine what type of food you want and how you will obtain it. Will it be a catered event? If so, you will need to secure a caterer and go through the necessary steps of checking prices, getting a contract, getting a check to pay the caterer, and so forth. Will you have students bring in homemade dishes? If so, you will need to create a sign-up sheet with the various types of food—salad, side dish, main course, dessert, bread, etc.—and have members sign up to bring a dish. Whichever method you choose, determine how much time each of these steps will take. Plan backwards from the date of the event and schedule deadlines by which you must accomplish each step.

PowerPoint presentation. To achieve the objective of having a motivational PowerPoint presentation of candid photos of staff members, you must set dates by which members will take photos, select and obtain the music that will accompany the presentation, and put the show together. You must also submit requests for the necessary audio/visual equipment.

Servers. To achieve the objective of having student servers at the event, you must recruit students to help, devise a schedule, and assign people to work at the various stations you need.

Invitations. To achieve the objective of having faculty and staff members attend the event, you must let them know about it. Will you put an announcement in the faculty bulletin? If so, what is the deadline for submitting the announcement? Will you create individual invitations? If so, when do you plan to put them in teacher mailboxes? Back up from that target date and give yourself time to create a design, obtain supplies, and get them made or photocopied. Who will stuff the mailboxes? When?

Standardize the Process

Working through the example of the faculty lunch helps illustrate backwards planning, but how can you standardize this process for use with other projects? The General Checklist for Activity Planning (see page 26) and the Project Planning form (see page 28) can help student leaders work through the various elements involved in planning any project and help them consider aspects they might not think of on their own. Once student leaders have done this, they should create a master schedule of tasks and deadlines, and who is responsible for them. To keep track of these details and ensure that nothing is overlooked, list all the tasks, assignments, and deadlines on a standard form such as the Task Assignment sheet (see page 30). Committee chairs, officers, and the adviser can refer to the sheet to refresh their memory of any details and keep everyone on task. Other forms, such as the Publicity Planning sheet on page 32, can help student leaders think through all the elements needed for their project.

Committees

Committees are a vital element in a successful student organization. Wherever and whenever there is a task that can't be handled by one or two people in a short period of time, a committee is likely to be formed. Committees make big jobs manageable by breaking them into smaller segments and involve more people in the group's activities by assigning people to be responsible for those segments. The result is greater efficiency and a stronger group.

Reasons for Forming Committees

There are many reasons for setting up committees, regardless of the tasks they are to complete. In the earlier example of a faculty appreciation lunch, an overall committee organized to plan the lunch might break up into sub-committees for each of the areas outlined: decorations, food, PowerPoint presentation, servers, and invitations. Spreading the work out in this manner helps involve more people in the group's activities so they feel ownership in its projects. It also enables your group to use the talent and abilities of a larger group of student leaders and avoid overusing its officers.

Committees are useful for a variety of other reasons:

• Committees allow group leaders to use the talents of group members to best advantage by assigning them to committees where their specialized skills can be utilized.

• By selecting people to serve on committees who ran for office but weren't elected, or others who have good leadership skills who perhaps weren't interested in running for an office, your group can develop the talent and abilities of a larger group of student leaders and avoid overusing its officers.

• Committee work is an excellent opportunity to provide training to younger members of the group so they can gain experience and confidence to serve as officers or chairs when they become upperclassmen.

• A committee can save time for the larger group by discussing and eliminating impractical ideas and by selecting the most relevant, valuable ideas to recommend to the organization for action.

Types of Committees

Committees are formed for specific purposes and may be used to:

• Plan specific activities

• Brainstorm about a project

• Present the best ideas to the large group

• Investigate issues and report the findings to the large group

- Perform specific work (sell tickets, clean up after a dance, etc.)
- Get more done in less time by delegating responsibilities
- Represent the organization at official functions.

Because there are many different purposes for committees, there are different kinds of committees:

Standing committees are defined as those committees appointed or elected for an entire year. Their work is not necessarily limited to one project. An example of a standing committee is a committee appointed or elected to plan all student assemblies for the school year. A standing committee might use several special committees throughout the year to do the actual work on each assembly. Other typical standing committees include membership, service projects, spirit, and elections.

Special committees (often called *ad hoc committees*) are appointed for a specific purpose and once they have accomplished their goal, they disband. A Spring Fling dance committee is an example of a special committee that would plan and do the work for one event—the dance. Special committees are assigned specific responsibilities that should be practical, reasonable, and clearly stated. If the committee members are unclear about what their assignments are, the chairperson should immediately seek clarification from the vice president or officer assigned to committee coordination.

Executive committees are made up of officers, committee chairpersons, or an elected board. They plan large group meetings and initiate and organize activities. Often this group recommends the formation of standing or special committees to carry out the plans it makes. The executive committee reviews major items and makes recommendations before going to the entire group.

Committee Functions

Regardless of what *type* of committee is formed—standing, special, or executive—each committee also has a particular function. For example, a special committee's job might be to advise, to coordinate, or to get specific work done.

- *Advisory committees* are formed to study a problem, report back to the large group with facts and figures, and make recommendations.
- *Coordinating committees* are convened to lay out a general plan or direction, to act as a liaison with other committees, or perhaps as an "umbrella" committee that coordinates the operation of special committees, such as the Homecoming Steering committee.
- *Work committees* have a specific job to complete or goal to accomplish.

Some committees perform several of these functions at different points.

Forming a Committee

A committee will not work unless all the members know what they are supposed to do and are committed to getting it done. When forming a committee, the following questions should be answered:

- What is the purpose of the committee?

- What are its responsibilities and limitations?

- What are the specific tasks to be accomplished?

- When should the job be completed and what type of report is expected?

- What is the role of officers and how is the membership of the committee to be decided?

- What is the term of office for members, method of filling vacancies, and method for appointing the chair?

- What is the authority of the committee?

- Is there a budget?

- What resources are needed? What resources are already available?

Committee members may be appointed, chosen from volunteers, or elected by the members of the entire group. The committee should be a congenial group, yet represent several points of view. Its size may vary according to the project and the scope of work to be accomplished. Obviously, a committee decorating a hall for a dance will have more members than a committee that is investigating the cost of bands. Smaller groups often work more effectively, although in some situations it is better to have too many people on a committee than too few, as is the case with a committee assigned the job of cleaning up after a school rally.

Some general rules about committee size are:

- The ideal size for groups attempting to discuss and develop ideas is between five and seven people. With fewer than five people, the variety of perspectives needed is not available; with more than seven people, members may become frustrated because of the number of others who also want to speak.

- Members of a working committee should have enough to keep busy. People who show up to work on an assignment but find nothing to do may be reluctant to become involved again.

- Members should not be overworked—the quality of their project diminishes, and they may not want to help in the future.

Selecting a Chair

The committee chair is the key leader of all committee work. This person should be selected after careful consideration by the organization. Choose someone who is interested and can work easily with others. The chair's role is not necessarily one of bringing technical expertise to the group. The fact that a person is a good artist does not mean that he or she will be good at chairing the publicity committee. The chair must be organized and know how to organize both programs and people. He or she must know how to involve others and motivate them to do the work of the committee.

The chairperson has the final responsibility for the success of the committee and must

Ideas to Generate Participation in Committees

After a committee has been in operation for a while, sometimes it loses momentum and members lose interest. To increase attendance and participation in committee meetings, consider some or all of the following:

- Ensure that committee chairs understand and can convey the role of the committee to members, and that the chair and members have up-to-date job descriptions.

- Let go of "dead wood." It often helps to decrease the number of committee members rather than increase them.

- Consider using subcommittees to increase individual responsibilities and focus on goals.

- Attempt to provide individual assignments to the committee members.

- Develop a committee attendance policy that specifies the number of times a member can be absent in consecutive meetings and in total meetings per time period.

- Generate minutes for each committee meeting to get closure on items and help members comprehend the progress made by the committee.

work with the members to decide WHAT has to be done, WHO will do it, WHERE it will be done, and WHEN it must be completed. The chairperson also needs to know and communicate how much authority the committee has. (See specific duties on page 14.)

Selecting the Members

A willingness to serve on a committee and do the work is often the only trait student leaders look for when making up the membership of their committees. Some other traits to look for in committee members include:

- Willingness to consider other points of view

- Willingness to drop an argument for the sake of moving ahead with the bigger issues

- Alert listening and honest questioning

- Ability to think logically

- Talents that mesh with those of other committee members

- Ability to follow through on assignments

- Time management skills.

Committee members also have important responsibilities. Without their dedication, the committee will fail. Good committee members must:

- Know the purpose of the committee

- Understand the specific task they have been assigned

- Attend all the meetings

- Participate in planning, share ideas, ask questions

- Commit to completing their work on time

- Keep track of supplies used, money spent, etc.

- Be respectful of the chairperson and other members

- Keep the full committee up-to-date on the tasks they have been assigned.

The Committee Report

When a committee's work is done or a specific project is finished, a final report should be written and filed for future reference. Develop a standard form (see page 31) for chairs to complete and ask them to attach supplemental documentation such as letters sent or received, receipts, instruction sheets, publicity plans, and so forth. These committee reports will provide invaluable information to future officers and committee chairs as they undertake similar activities.

General Checklist for Activity Planning

The steps involved in planning an activity will vary depending on the type of activity. Review the following list and check the items needed for your event.

Name of Event: _____

Administrative

❑ Obtain administrative approval for the activity

❑ Put the activity date on the school calendar

❑ Make arrangements to reserve needed facilities (gym, cafeteria, etc.)

❑ Submit requests for custodial assistance

    ❑ Chairs   ❑ Tables

    ❑ Risers   ❑ Podium

    ❑ Trash cans   ❑ Other:

Audio/Visual needs

❑ Microphone

❑ Sound system

❑ Lights (spotlight, stage lights, etc.)

❑ Projector (LCD, slide, movie, etc.)

❑ MP3 or CD player

❑ Other:

Decorations

❑ Select theme

❑ Order decorations

❑ Organize people to decorate

❑ Gather supplies for decorating: tape, scissors, air pumps, staplers, trash cans, etc.

Tickets

❑ Determine admission/ticket price

❑ Design ticket

❑ Arrange for tickets to be printed

❑ Schedule ticket sales workers

❑ Arrange for cash box for ticket sales

❑ Arrange for depositing money from sales

Publicity

❑ Design and create posters, fliers, table tents

❑ Create PA announcements

❑ Draft press release and deliver to local media

❑ Send invitations to special guests

❑ Alert yearbook/newspaper staff to have a photographer at the event

❑ Other:

Program

❑ Create schedule of events

❑ Contract with entertainment (band/DJ, speaker, games equipment, etc.)

❑ Request checks to pay for contracted services (band/DJ, security, caterer, etc.)

❑ Schedule rehearsal

❑ Design printed program

❑ Arrange for program to be printed

❑ Determine program distribution method (on chairs, hand out, etc.) and recruit workers

Refreshments

❑ Order refreshments or contract with caterer

❑ Arrange for ice, tables, etc., for refreshments

❑ Obtain necessary supplies: cups, plates, napkins, eating utensils, serving utensils, etc.

❑ Organize servers for refreshment distribution

❑ Arrange for a cash box if selling refreshments

Chaperones/Security

❑ Request administrative supervision

❑ Recruit chaperones

❑ Create a schedule of work stations and list of duties for chaperones

❑ Create chart for layout of event and traffic flow

❑ Create a token of appreciation for chaperones or write thank-you notes

❑ Hire security guards for parking lot patrol

Judging/Contests

❑ Determine criteria for judging

❑ Recruit judges

❑ Create judging sheets

❑ Determine and obtain prizes

❑ Write thank-you notes to judges

Follow Up

❑ Organize clean-up effort

❑ Conduct evaluation

❑ Write and send thank-you notes

❑ Complete reports for the files

General Planning Notes:

Project Planning

Name of Project:_____

Chairperson:_____ Overall goal this project supports:_____

Date, time, location of project:_____

Purpose of project: ○ Tradition   ○ Social   ○ Service   ○ Spirit   ○ Fundraiser   ○ Other

Visualize the project as you would like it to be. What will it consist of?

_____

_____

_____

List three goals you want to achieve with this project.

1. _____

2. _____

3 _____

Checklist: Do you need any of the following? If so, describe on the back of this form.

○ Administrative approval   ○ Prizes

○ Master calendar request   ○ Special guest invitations

○ Facility request   ○ Audio/visual equipment

○ Custodial arrangements   ○ Special equipment

○ Legal contracts   ○ Set-up/clean-up crew

○ Check requests   ○ Work schedule

○ Cash box   ○ Decorations

○ Tickets   ○ Refreshments

○ Chaperones/Security   ○ Printed program

○ Judges   ○ Other:_____

Publicity: What types of publicity do you need?

○ Posters   ○ Bulletin boards

○ PA announcements   ○ Press release

○ Fliers   ○ In-school TV/radio commercial

○ Table tents   ○ Community access cable

○ Website item   ○ Twitter/Facebook/YouTube item

○ E-mails   ○ Other (be creative!): _____

Budget: How much money do you have to work with? _____

Do you have necessary approval to spend money?   ○ Yes   ○ No

Materials: List all materials or equipment needed.

Item	Source	Cost

Task Assignment Sheet

List each task to be done, who is responsible for completing it, and a deadline for completion.

Task to be completed	Who's doing it?	By when?

Form completed by: _____   Date: _____

Committee Report

Name of Committee: _____

Committee Assignment: _____

_____

Key Discussion Points:

Action Items:

Recommendations and/or Points for Further Discussion:

Names of Committee Members Attending Meeting:

Meeting Date:_____ Signature of Chair: _____

Publicity Planning

Event name: _____

Date: _____ Time: _____ Place: _____

Special theme, logo, or colors that should be used: _____

Budget for publicity: _____ Date publicity should begin:_____

Will tickets be needed?   ◯ Yes   ◯ No

   On sale when? _____ On sale where? _____

   Ticket price: _____ Sales start: _____ Sales end:_____

What audience do we want to reach?
   ◯ Students   ◯ Parents   ◯ Faculty/staff   ◯ Community   ◯ Other

Methods we will use to reach our audiences: Who will be responsible:

◯ Bulletin/PA announcements   _____

◯ Posters   _____

◯ Marquee or electronic message board   _____

◯ Fliers   _____

◯ Table tents   _____

◯ Chalkboard/whiteboard notices   _____

◯ Sidewalk chalking   _____

◯ Locker signs   _____

◯ Yard signs   _____

◯ Press release   _____

◯ Radio PSAs   _____

◯ Website item   _____

◯ Blast e-mail or text message   _____

◯ YouTube, Facebook, or Twitter item   _____

◯ Newsletter item   _____

◯ Bulletin board   _____

◯ In-school TV/radio ad   _____

◯ Community access cable   _____

◯ Other (be creative!):   _____

Write any additional information, ideas, or suggestions on the back of this form.

Chapter 3

MEETING MANAGEMENT

IN THIS CHAPTER

- Planning and Conducting Meetings
- Meeting Minutes
- Meeting Techniques

- Facilitating Comments
- Meeting Planning Forms

Meetings are an important aspect of student activity work. With limited time to meet and often conflicting demands on members, it is essential that meeting time be put to good use. The first meeting of your organization is especially important as it will set the tone for meetings to come and will influence the participation of members. If the initial meeting is well organized and clearly directed, members will be more likely to want to continue to participate; a poorly run meeting will leave them wondering what they've gotten themselves into.

Planning and Conducting Meetings

All of your organization's meetings should have a well-thought-out plan that will help ensure that group goals are reached.

Although meetings take many forms and serve many purposes, they all share some common elements. When planning and conducting meetings, take the following steps to ensure that members leave feeling their time was well spent.

■ *Define the purpose of the meeting.* All meetings should have specific reasons for bringing people together. If there is no real reason, don't hold the meeting! Sometimes the purpose is clearly stated; sometimes it's taken for granted. Do you want people to experience something? Learn something? Decide something? Plan something? Consider various activities that will help accomplish your purpose and structure your meeting to accomplish the purpose you have in mind.

■ *Plan the agenda.* Once you know your

objective, develop a written outline of the items to be handled during the meeting. List them in the order in which they are to be addressed, indicate how long will be spent on each item, and who will be handling each item. Also consider what method will be used for each item, such as presentations, brainstorming, buzz groups, etc. Place items on the agenda in order of priority so if time runs short you will have covered the most important items (see form on page 43).

Many groups follow a simple version of the order of business recommended in *Robert's Rules of Order*. Items are usually handled in this order:

- Call to order
- Roll call (to determine if a quorum is present)
- Reading and approval of minutes (see sample on page 36)
- Treasurer's report (see sidebar)
- Reports by other officers of work done since the previous meeting
- Reports by committees of work done since the previous meeting
- Unfinished business—including items left over from previous meetings or any questions that were pending at the last session when it was adjourned
- New business—new items of business or motions to be considered. If more information or action is required, the item can be left unfinished and be taken up under old business at the next meeting.

- Announcements about committee meetings or other items of interest
- Program (an optional speaker or other informative program)
- Recap of next steps/tasks assigned
- Adjournment.

Some meetings call for a less formal agenda than the one listed above. Even a committee meeting or a quick meeting of officers should have some idea of the specific results group members want to obtain. If an agenda

Sample Treasurer's Report

A treasurer's report is an itemized listing of the money that has come in and gone out of the treasury since the last report. Start by listing the balance given in the last report, then list each deposit made, expenses paid, and the new balance. The report will look something like this:

Treasurer's Report October 14

Balance as of September 14	$546.77

Income:

Receipts from back-to-school mixer:	$830.00
Receipts from lollygram sale:	$535.00

Disbursements:

Soda and candy for mixer refreshments	$76.89
Candy for lollygrams	$211.17
Fall conference registration	$150.00
Current balance:	$1,473.71

hasn't been developed before the meeting, develop one on the spot at the start of the meeting so everyone knows what will be covered.

■ *Consider your time limit.* Times of meetings vary greatly. How much can be dealt with in the time available? An over-ambitious agenda is easy to fall into and sets the group up to fall short of its goals, leaving some members frustrated because their business was not dealt with. Plan your agenda so that everything can be handled within the time allowed.

■ *Plan for the people who will be involved*. Who will be leading the activities? Before the meeting, share the agenda with the people involved so they can be prepared to give reports, discuss topics, and share opinions. Be sure they are aware of their time allotments.

Also consider who will be present at the meeting. Are they familiar with the business at hand? If not, how can you bring them up to speed? How motivated will they be to participate?

■ *Schedule the meeting in an appropriate setting.* Plan an atmosphere that will be conducive to participation and productivity. Consider such things as size of room, seating arrangement, lighting, acoustics, temperature, and equipment needed. For example, if your objective is to get small groups of people together to discuss an issue and come up with potential solutions, you wouldn't want to hold the meeting in the auditorium, where small group discussions are awkward at best. Hold it instead in the library or cafeteria where groups can gather around a table.

If possible, it's a good idea to find a regular meeting place for committee meetings and large group meetings so members will become accustomed to going to the same place and won't have to figure out each time where the meeting is to be held.

Be sure to complete any necessary room reservations so there will be no conflict with another group trying to use the facility at the same time.

■ *Make arrangements for equipment.* Check to be sure that any equipment needed (microphone, slide or LCD projector, video player, blackboard, flip chart, markers, etc.) will be available.

■ *Prepare paperwork.* Prepare and make photocopies for participants of committee reports, minutes of previous meetings, the agenda, a meeting evaluation form, and any other handouts.

■ *Notify participants.* Be sure to inform all members of the meeting's date, starting time, and location. If possible, follow up with a personal contact, phone call, or e-mail reminder.

■ *Start the meeting on time.* Few things are as frustrating as sitting around for 15 or 20 minutes waiting for all the members to arrive. If this happens, people will get the idea that punctuality isn't important and subsequent meetings will have the same

Meeting Minutes

Minutes are a record of what was done, not what was said. Minutes should be kept in a permanent record book or notebook for later reference. A standard format for meeting minutes calls for the following information to be included:

- Kind of meeting (regular, special, called, etc.)
- Name of group or committee
- Date, time, and place of meeting
- Members in attendance
- Minutes read and statement of approval or amendment
- All main motions and their disposition
- Time of adjournment and name of recorder.

Having a form that is completed by people making motions at a meeting will make the secretary's job easier and help ensure that the minutes are accurate. (See page 44.)

Distributing the minutes to members in written form as people enter the meeting can save time during the meeting. At the appropriate time, the chair asks "are there any corrections or additions to the minutes?" If there are none, the chair asks for a motion to approve the minutes as written. Otherwise, make the necessary changes and the chair then asks for a motion to approve the minutes as corrected.

Sample Minutes of a Student Council Meeting

The regular meeting of the Lynwood Student Council met on Tuesday, September 21, 2010 at 2:45 in Room 230. The meeting was called to order by president Robby Allen. There were 24 members present and 3 members absent.

Alaina Page, secretary, called the roll and read the minutes of the previous meeting, which were approved as read. Treasurer David Pearson reported a balance of $1,473.71.

The dance committee chair, Ian Aumer, reported on the success of the back to school mixer. Fundraising chair, Staci Yeager, reported on the success of the fall lollygram sale.

In new business, it was moved by Kyle Preston and seconded that the Lynwood Student Council sponsor a teacher appreciation luncheon on November 16, 2010. Motion carried. President Allen appointed Kyle to chair the committee for this event.

It was moved by Adam Richards and seconded that the council participate in Freedom's Answer. President Allen appointed Madelyn Wingard to chair the effort.

The meeting was adjourned at 3:57 p.m.

Respectfully submitted by Alaina Page, Secretary

problem. By starting on time, you send the message that you value people's time and their commitment to being there. Latecomers will realize they need to make more of an effort to be punctual in the future.

■ *Follow your plan.* Work through the agenda items one at a time, being careful to stick to time limits and avoid getting off track. Be flexible enough to adjust your plan if truly needed, but don't allow one item to take over the meeting unless it's warranted.

■ *Work as a facilitator.* Much of the success of an effective meeting depends on the skills of the leader. Stay neutral. Work to involve all members of the group in discussion and cultivate an atmosphere of free exchange of ideas, remembering that the leader need not comment on every contribution. When general and abstract problems are proposed, ask for specific examples or suggestions. Do not let meetings drag; move business along when discussion gets repetitious. Summarize often, bringing together the areas upon which all in the group members have agreed and suggesting proposals and considerations on all sides.

■ *Review decisions made.* All agreements made during the meeting should be verified at the end of the meeting, such as tasks assigned, chairs appointed, committees formed, etc. Plan steps that need to be taken before the next meeting to advance projects undertaken. Before you adjourn, set dates to report progress on each assignment and agree upon a date and time for the next meeting.

■ *Evaluate the meeting.* Take a few minutes at the end of the meeting to evaluate its success. What went well? What could be improved upon for the next meeting? Focusing on the process will help all members have a better understanding of what a good meeting should be like and help ensure that each meeting is more effective than the last.

Meeting Techniques

Many management techniques can be used, depending on the type of meeting being held. No single technique works for all situations.

Parliamentary Procedure

Parliamentary procedure is an effective tool to facilitate large group meetings and provides a sound basis for democratic decision making. Parliamentary procedure protects the rights of both the majority and the minority. The majority has the right to prevail on any given issue and the right to reasonable expediency in arriving at a decision. The minority has the right to be heard and the right to attempt to persuade others to accept its viewpoint (thus converting a temporary minority into a majority).

The fundamental principles of parliamentary procedure are:

• Rules exist to promote cooperation and harmony.

• All members have equal rights, privileges, and obligations.

• The vote of the majority decides.

• The minority has rights that must be protected.

Advantages and Disadvantages of Parliamentary Procedure

Advantages of Parliamentary Procedure

1. Justice and courtesy are extended to each person.
2. Only one item of business is considered at a time.
3. The majority opinion is maintained.
4. The rights of the minority are respected.
5. This is the oldest and best-known technique for conducting business.
6. Meetings that utilize parliamentary procedure are more focused and orderly.

Disadvantages of Parliamentary Procedure

1. It may become so complicated that it obstructs, restrains, or hinders group discussion or action.
2. It is not universally known or understood; it needs to be taught to members.
3. It may not be the best technique for generating ideas and suggestions in regard to the problems involved.
4. It does not encourage creativity.
5. People who know it well can manipulate discussion to gain advantage over those who don't know it.

- Full discussion of all propositions is a right.
- Logical precedence governs introduction and disposition of motions.
- One question/item of business is considered at a time.

The heart of parliamentary procedure is the motion, a proposal by a member of the group that the group take certain action. Any member may make a motion. Motions should be stated in positive terms. The correct wording is to say, "I move that …" NOT "I motion that …." Motions must be seconded—"I second the motion" —to show that at least two members are interested in the proposal. If there is no second, the motion dies. There can be no discussion, no vote.

The will of the group on this matter must be determined before another main question may be considered. The group may express its will on the proposed course of action by adopting it, rejecting it, amending it, delaying it, or suppressing it.

Members who wish to discuss the motion must rise, address the chair, and be recognized. Members generally speak only once and limit their remarks to pertinent comments. During discussion, members may make subsidiary motions to alter or change the disposition of the main motion. Such motions include motions to amend, table, refer to committee, limit debate, or postpone. Any subsidiary motions must be addressed before the main motion can be voted on.

When discussion lags, the chairperson may call for a vote saying, "Are you ready for the question?" If no one objects, the chair puts the motion to vote by saying, "It has been moved and seconded that …. All in favor of the motion say 'aye'. All those opposed say 'no'." The chair then announces the results: "The motion is carried," or "The motion has failed." If the chair is not sure of the vote, he or she may ask for a show of hands, a standing vote, or a roll call vote.

This is a basic overview of parliamentary procedure. For more thorough information, check *Parliamentary Procedure Without Stress* and other resources listed in the appendix.

Parliamentary Procedure Primer

If You Want To:	Say This:
• Introduce business to the group for consideration	"I move to…"
• Indicate that you support consideration of another member's motion	"I second the motion."
• Alter a motion as it was originally presented	"I move to amend the motion by …"
• Further investigate or have someone study in more depth	"I move that we refer this matter to committee."
• Delay action to a specific time	"I move to postpone action on this matter until…"
• Postpone action for more pressing business until later in the meeting or until the next meeting	"I move to table the motion."
• Bring the meeting focus back to the agenda	"I call for the orders of the day," or "I move that we consider the topic on the agenda, namely …"
• Stop debate and call for a vote	"I move the previous question."
• Verify a voice vote by hand, standing, or roll call vote	"I call for a division of the house."
• Reconsider an issue (may only be made by a person who voted on the prevailing side)	"I voted with the prevailing side of the motion which (state motion) and move to reconsider the action taken," or "…move to have the matter reconsidered at the next meeting."
• Close meeting	"I move we adjourn."

Interaction Method

The Interaction Method is a trademarked approach to building understanding and agreement among groups of people. Elements of this method include:

• Shared responsibility—the principle that everyone in the group can play an active and positive role in producing meaningful results.

• A collaborative attitude—the mindset that guides individuals to act in a cooperative manner.

• Facilitative behaviors—the practical techniques and actions that help people to build understanding and agreement.

• Strategic focus—the mental process of selecting an appropriate course of action to achieve desired results. (Source: *www.interactionassociates.com/html/interaction_method.html*)

The Interaction Method uses a facilitator and recorder to post the group agenda, create ground rules, and help with interaction and participation. The facilitator keeps the group focused and on track. The recorder writes down group member ideas on butcher paper, posted so people can clearly see their recorded words. This is an effective method to foster participation of all members of the group and to build consensus by sharing ownership of plans.

Action Planning

This informal strategy helps groups make plans to achieve goals, handle a situation, or solve a problem. It's a logical, step-by-step process that includes discussion of these things:

• Goal—a sentence or brief paragraph that states one goal in concise, easy-to-understand terms. This is the end you want to achieve.

• Capacity—an inventory of the resources that can be committed to the goal, such as money, expertise, volunteers, etc. Demonstrate that the resources are sufficient to execute the goal.

• Payoff—the expected benefits that will result from achieving the goal. Be specific.

• Risk—the possible down side of undertaking this goal. What will be lost if the group fails in its attempt? Is the group willing to bear the risk?

• Strategy—one or more statements of what needs to be accomplished to achieve the goal.

• Tasks—for each strategy, a list that details the specific activities to be undertaken to carry out the strategy. What is the task? Who will do it? When will it be completed? The key element is to define who will do what when.

Buzz Groups

Buzz groups are a good way to allow all members to discuss an issue or consider a specific question in a time-efficient manner. Divide the large group into small groups of four to eight persons. Each group may consider the same question, or give each group a different aspect of a particular issue to discuss. Each group selects a leader and a recorder. At the end of an allotted period of time, the leader of each buzz group presents the group's report to the whole group. In this way, every individual takes an active role in the discussion and everyone has an opportunity for their voice to be heard, albeit with a limited number of people.

Facilitating Comments

To promote clear communication and help make sure that the purpose of the meeting is accomplished, a good facilitator needs to summarize what has been said—and what is occurring that is unsaid—in the meeting. The following comments can be helpful when facilitating a group:

- "Let's check that out with the rest of the group."
- "Do you see it differently?"
- "How do you see the problem?"
- "Sounds like that's a problem we ought to address."
- "I still don't have a handle on the real problem. What is it?"
- Boomerang—"What would *you* like to be doing?"
- "Oh, your perception is…(describe). That's how you see the problem."
- "Sounds like this is a real problem."
- "Looks like you're really concerned about this issue."
- "Feels like we're wasting valuable time. What would be a better use of our time?"
- Feeding back what is going on— "Sounds like you're all worn out."
- "What are we doing right now?"
- "Say a little more about that."
- "What's the purpose of this presentation?"
- "Hold on. I think we're talking about two problems, problem _____ and problem _____. I think they are both important, but let's talk about them one at a time.
- "It's a big agenda today. Do you want to get through the whole agenda? (yes) Okay, if I push too hard, let me know."
- "What do you want to have happen?"
- "Wait a second. We're jumping all around. We're brainstorming, discussing, clarifying, and debating. Let's stay in one phase at a time."
- "That's an important consideration. Let's get that down. I'd like to come back to that after we finish the subject we're on, okay?"

Excerpted from the *National Leadership Camp Curriculum Guide* © 1994 NASSP, pages 128–130.

Planning a Meeting Checklist

Every meeting should have a well-thought-out plan to help ensure that goals are reached. Although meetings take many forms and serve many purposes, they all share some things in common. When planning the meeting, take the following items into consideration to ensure a productive experience.

Before the Meeting

❏ Determine if there is a need for a meeting.

❏ Establish who should participate—whole organization, committee, officers only, etc.

❏ Determine the best time and day to hold the meeting.

❏ Reserve the meeting room or verify the meeting place availability during the time set for the meeting so there will be no conflict with another group trying to use the facility.

❏ Prepare a preliminary agenda with time estimates of how long each agenda item will take.

❏ Identify who will lead activities or present information during the meeting and discuss with them what is expected.

❏ Notify members well in advance of the time, date, and location of the meeting.

❏ Send letters of invitation to guest speakers or other nonmembers who are to attend the meeting. Include map or directions.

❏ Prepare copies of the agenda, previous minutes, committee reports, or other handouts for attendees.

❏ Make room set-up or custodial arrangements and check that appropriate number of chairs, tables, etc. are available.

❏ Test necessary equipment (microphone, slide projector, video player, etc.) to make sure it works and it's in the right location.

❏ Arrange the tables and chairs into a configuration conducive to the planned activities.

❏ Check the layout of the room to make sure everyone can see all speakers and visual aids.

❏ Order refreshments.

❏ Prepare visual aids.

❏ Prepare meeting evaluation form or activity.

❏ Arrange for greeters to stand at entrance to help with questions.

During the Meeting

❏ Start the meeting on time.

❏ Welcome attendees and make introductions as needed.

❏ Follow the agenda and keep the meeting moving.

❏ Encourage participation by all attendees.

❏ Keep discussion on the topic; if new items come up, hold them for another meeting.

❏ Review decisions made and action items at the end of the meeting.

❏ Assign follow-up action items to specific members.

❏ Evaluate the meeting for what worked, what didn't work, and what could have gone better.

❏ Schedule the next meeting time.

After The Meeting

❏ Clean up the facility.

❏ Return equipment.

❏ Send thank-you notes to those who helped.

❏ Read and analyze meeting evaluation forms to see what could be done better next time.

❏ Prepare minutes of the meeting and distribute to everyone who attended.

❏ E-mail or phone to remind people of follow-up.

❏ Make plans for the next meeting.

Agenda Planning

Meeting: _____

Date: _____

Time: _____

Place: _____

Agenda Item	Who's Responsible?	Time Estimate

Motions

Anyone making a motion at a meeting should complete this form and give it to the secretary prior to the vote on the motion. This will help ensure the accuracy of the minutes.

Name of person making the motion: _____

Motion seconded by: _____

Exact wording of motion:_____

_____

_____

_____

_____

_____

Disposition of motion: ❏ passed   ❏ failed   ❏ tabled

Meeting Minutes

Group: _____ Date: _____

Call to order by: _____ Time of meeting: _____ Place of meeting: _____

Presiding officer: _____ Roll call by: _____

# of Members present _____ # of Members absent: _____

Reading of minutes by: _____

Minutes were ❏ approved as read ❏ amended

Reports

Officers: _____

Committees: _____

Unfinished business

Item: _____

Action taken: _____

Item: _____

Action taken: _____

New business

❶ Motion made & by whom: _____

Major points of discussion: _____

Action taken: votes for: _____ votes against: _____

❷ Motion made & by whom: _____

Major points of discussion: _____

Action taken: votes for: _____ votes against: _____

❸ Motion made & by whom: _____

Major points of discussion: _____

Action taken: votes for: _____ votes against: _____

Announcements: _____

Adjournment at: _____

Committee Meeting Minutes

Committee Name: _____ Date of meeting:_____

Members present: _____

_____

Minutes submitted by: _____

Chapter 4

FINANCIAL MANAGEMENT

Financial management is an area in which advisers should take particular care. No adviser wants his or her management of organization funds called into question. Learning about and carefully following school policies on handling student funds is the safest course.

Policies for Management of Funds

When you become a student activity adviser, make an appointment to meet with the school's bookkeeper or district business manager to go over policies governing management of organization funds and fundraising. Be sure to get answers to the following questions:

- Is a vote of the membership required to approve expenditure of funds?

- Are purchase orders required for purchases? If so, what is the procedure for getting a purchase order approved and how long does it take?

- What is the procedure for requesting a check?

- What is the procedure for requesting a cash box with change?

- Is there a reimbursement policy?

- What procedures govern depositing money?

- What type of record keeping is required?

- Does the district provide numbered receipt books?

- Does the district provide a regular statement of account to the adviser? How often?

- What are the fundraising policies? Is there a limit to how many fundraising projects you can have? What types of fundraisers are allowed? What is the process for getting a fundraiser approved?

- Are there any other guidelines or policies that you should be aware of?

Developing a Budget

A budget is a financial plan of action that estimates what your expenses and income will be. Organizations that handle money should never try to operate without a budget. The group should have an overall budget for the year, and each activity or project should have its own budget.

Project Budgets

It's important for each committee chair to operate within a budget. Without a guideline of how much money is available for the project, it's easy to go overboard on expenses. For example, the Spring Fling committee might like to spend money on leis, tropical decorations, and free pineapple drinks for everyone who attends, but without first estimating how much money the Spring Fling mixer is likely to bring in, they won't know if they have the money to do what they plan.

To create a project budget, follow these steps:

■ **Look at previous expenses and income as a guide.** If the event has been held before, check organization files to see how many people attended and what the expenses were.

If it's a new event, estimate expenses and income from similar events, or make your best guess.

■ **Estimate revenue.** How much money will the activity likely bring in? Consider all sources of revenue, including ticket sales (advance and at the door), concessions, ad revenue from programs, donations, and so forth. As part of estimating ticket sales, calculate how many people can be expected to participate in the activity; you will need this figure for estimating expenses.

■ **Estimate expenses.** Consider all the areas in which your group will have expenses.

- Will there be rental fees for the site or equipment?

- Will refreshments be served? If so, figure costs for the food and drink and also cups, napkins, plates, etc.

- What publicity costs are involved? Will you need to buy poster-making supplies, run off fliers, print tickets, make programs?

- Are decorations needed? If so, list each item and its cost.

- Will there be contracted entertainment, such as a DJ?

- Will there be prizes or awards? Sometimes donations can be obtained for these, but if you are awarding ribbons or plaques, the cost must be factored in.

- How will you thank people who have helped with the event? The cost of flowers or a fruit basket for a faculty member who really helped, or small candy bars to accompany thank-you notes should be part of the budget.

■ **Compare estimated expenses with estimated revenue.** For most projects, you want your revenue figures to be higher than your expenses. If they are not, you have two options. Either figure out how to trim expenses so they are in line with revenue, or figure out how to increase the revenue for the project (e.g., raising the ticket price, seeking donations for part of it, or selling ads for a program).

Occasionally, you will have projects that are worthwhile and advance the mission of your organization, but they don't bring in enough revenue to pay for themselves. In these cases, you must allow for this in other parts of your budget by making a profit elsewhere (see organization budgets below).

Organization Budgets

The overall budget for your organization will include all the activities and programs you plan to do for the coming year. In establishing the budget, keep in mind the stated purpose of your group. Your budget for activities and projects should reflect that purpose. Likewise, your expenditures should help you achieve your overall goals.

To create an organization budget, use the form on page 56 and follow these steps:

■ **Ask committee chairs to submit a budget report** from each of the committees and activities detailing what expenses they had and what revenues were generated.

■ **Scrutinize your expenditures and**

revenues **from the current year**. If you have a budget in place, compare the actual amounts against the estimates in your budget. How closely did expenses and revenues match up with what you planned for?

■ **Analyze the sources of revenue**. Have revenue sources changed from previous years? Are they sources you can count on in the future? What projects were ultimately the greatest revenue producers after expenses were met?

■ **Analyze the expenses for the year.** Are there ways to save money? For example, instead of buying balloons for each separate event, can you take advantage of quantity discounts and buy them all at once?

■ **Make a list of activities and programs that are likely to be undertaken next year.** Depending on when your group organizes its calendar for the year, it might be difficult to say with certainty which activities the group will sponsor. But there are often events that you can count on sponsoring. And after evaluating this year's activities, you might decide not to continue sponsoring others.

■ **Estimate revenue and expenses for next year.** Using figures from the budget reports for this year, extrapolate and forecast what is likely to happen next year. Plan for increased costs due to inflation by increasing your estimates by two or three percent over what was done this year.

■ **Account for non-revenue generating items** such as teacher appreciation items, attending workshops or conferences, membership in state or national organizations, general resources such as magazine subscriptions or books, and so forth. These things will need to be paid for with profits from those activities that generate a profit.

■ **Plan for a reserve amount** for unexpected items or projects and emergencies.

■ **Evaluate your proposed budget** to see how well it connects to the goals of your organization. Each budgeted item should tie to the organization's mission and goals. As the budget is developed, review each budget item and ask, "How does this relate what we want to accomplish as a group?"

■ **Compare total expected revenue to anticipated expenses.** If your expenses exceed revenue, you may need to prioritize the programs and activities you plan to sponsor. Which ones are most important to your organization's goals?

■ **Use the budget as a guide.** Once the budget is determined, use it as a guide as your organization goes about its business. Committee chairs can refer to it to know how much they can reasonably count on spending on various expenses, and officers can keep an eye on the bottom line to ensure that money is there to do all the activities the group has planned.

Record Keeping

Keeping an accurate and detailed account of expenses and income in your student activity account is important. Every time you receive or disburse funds, the transac-

tion should be recorded. Issue receipts for all money received. Deposit the money daily in the school vault. Issue checks for all money expended and keep supporting documents on file.

Many school districts provide a record-keeping book for organization accounting. If your district does not, purchase a bookkeeping ledger from an office supply store or use one of the software programs designed for this purpose. A simple spreadsheet program should suffice to keep track of all transactions.

A standard receipt book is also essential. This should be used to record all monies received by the organization. These receipts should be in duplicate with the carbon copy remaining in the organization's files and the original going to the person paying the money. This receipt file should be accurately maintained as proof of monies collected in case of audit or if proof is needed at any time.

Most school districts provide advisers with a monthly statement listing deposits and disbursements for organization accounts. Advisers should check this statement each month to ensure that organization records match official district reports and clear up any discrepancies immediately.

Training Your Treasurer

Some schools hold a training session for all organization treasurers so that everyone is using the same forms and following the same procedures. If your school doesn't do this, set up a meeting with your outgoing and incoming treasurers shortly after elections. Review rules, guidelines, school policies, and responsibilities.

Fundraising

While fundraising should never be the sole focus of a student organization, with ever-tightening school budgets in many schools it has become a necessary part of student activities to keep cocurricular programs going. Because most organizations will have to do at least one fundraiser during the year, turn the experience into a positive one by tying the effort to the purpose and goals of your group. Rather than simply conducting a sale of some item that is unrelated to your goals, consider how you could raise money and accomplish your goals at the same time.

For example, if one of your goals is to raise school spirit, brainstorm a list of fundraisers that could be related to school spirit. Perhaps you could sell bumper stickers, spirit ribbons, or school shirts. Perhaps you could have a spirit couch in a choice location at sporting events where students purchase a chance to sit with three of their friends and be served refreshments by members of your group. Relating your fundraising efforts to already established group goals enables you to get double the value for your efforts-- raise funds and accomplish goals at the same time!

Activity or Product?

Fundraising efforts can be divided into two main categories: sales campaigns in which a product of some sort is offered or activities where the main focus is an event or service for which you charge admission or another fee. Examples of each type include:

Activity Ideas

■ **Dances**. Many schools consistently make their best money with dances, while at others a dance is a sure way to lose money. One key to having a successful dance is to develop a theme and publicize it well. Some possible themes for casual dances include sponsoring a "Back to School Bash" at the beginning of the year, a "Jam Before You Cram" just before semester finals, a "Fifth Quarter" after a football or basketball game, or a "Spring Fever Reliever" in the spring. Keep your expenses down and generate as much attendance as you can to make holding a dance a worthwhile fundraiser.

■ **Game Show**. Organize an evening of game shows with students or faculty members as contestants and charge admission to the show. A "Wheel of Fortune" type game could be done with phrases selected by your group. Have teachers make up questions for a "Jeopardy" type quiz show or a take-off on "Are You Smarter Than a Fifth Grader" or "Who Wants to Be a Millionaire?" Set up obstacle courses in the gym for a version of "Wipe Out." For "Class Feud" have teams representing each grade level compete to answer survey questions about your school that 100 students have answered. Invite students from other schools to be contestants in a "Dating Game" or "Singled Out" format.

Fun Factor. Do a take-off of the "Fear Factor" television show using grade-level teams of students. Set up various fun events—instead of fearsome or risky ones—in the gym and charge admission to watch the fun.

Walk-in Movie. Rig a screen between the goal posts on the football field and show a popular movie. Allow people to bring blankets and beach chairs to sit on the field and watch the movie. Charge admission and sell refreshments.

Dive-in Movie. Pick a water-related movie (e.g., *Jaws*, *A Perfect Storm*, or *Waterworld*) and project it on the wall next to an indoor pool at school or in the community. Allow students to bring rafts and inner tubes to float on and watch the movie. Charge admission and sell refreshments (but create a designated area in which refreshments must be consumed to avoid problems with food getting in the pool!).

Your School Idol Contest. Solicit talented students to perform in a talent show set up like "American Idol." Draw a large crowd by recruiting a wide variety of students to perform—their friends and parents will come! Charge admission to the event.

Airband Contest or Battle of the Bands. Student bands or airbands compete to see which is voted the best. Judges are students, community members, local DJs, local musicians, the school's band director. Charge admission and sell refreshments.

Male Beauty Pageant. This is a spoof on beauty pageants with male contestants. Student organizations or classrooms nominate candidates who participate in beach wear, casual wear, formal wear, interview, and talent competitions. All contestants perform a choreographed dance together. The talent could be serious talent or could be items drawn out of a hat and performed extemporaneously, such as "do your best impression of Godzilla," or "pantomime sneaking in after curfew." Be sure to keep the focus on fun and don't allow offensive behavior such as cross-dressing or off-color comments. Charge admission to the show. Also, have contestants collect money and turn it in each day; the amounts they collect can be judged as one of the items that will determine who wins.

Dinner Theater. On the night of a school play, organize a dinner in the cafeteria before the play. Put tablecloths and candles on the tables and have student servers. An alternate idea is to have student one-act plays actually performed in the cafeteria while diners are eating.

Anything-a-Thon. Organize a marathon of anything you like—dancing, bowling, jumping rope, weight lifting, walking, rocking in a chair, you name it—and recruit participants who collect set contributions or pledges for the number of hours they participate or the number of times they do something.

Meal Deals. Spaghetti suppers, chili cook-offs, pancake breakfasts, barbeque picnics, and other events that involve a meal of some kind can be effective fundraisers. Get a local restaurant to sponsor the event and donate a percentage of each meal sold to your organization, or host the event yourself in the school cafeteria.

■ **Sports Tournaments**. Organize a sports tournament and charge teams a flat fee to participate. Softball, volleyball, basketball, golf, and bowling can all be profitable. Increase the fun by putting a twist on things: play volleyball in mud pits, do the bowling at midnight under neon lights, have faculty play against students, and so forth. Look for a local sporting goods store that might want to sponsor the event. Charge admission for spectators and sell refreshments.

Sales Ideas

■ **Merchandise Sales**. Many fundraising companies offer candy, wrapping paper, magazines, pizza, cookie dough, and other products for sale, with your organization getting a percentage of the total sales. To boost your success, sell something that people would buy anyway, such as wrapping paper before the holidays or plants in the spring.

■ **Candy Grams**. Prepare miniature cards (about ¼ of an 8 ½ x 11" piece of card-stock) with some sort of seasonal design and sell them for 25 or 50 cents. Buyers write personal messages on them, address them to a person at the school, and turn the completed cards back in to be delivered with candy on a specified day and time. These are often effective around holidays or other big

events such as Homecoming. Names and candy can be varied to fit the theme: Ghost Grams, Turkey Grams, Santa Grams, Heart Grams, Kiss a Friend Goodbye Grams, etc.

■ **Balloon Grams**. This works like candy grams but helium-filled balloons are delivered instead of candy. These must be sold for a higher price to cover the cost of materials and still make a profit.

■ **Flower Grams.** This works like candy and balloon grams, but with flowers. Different color flowers can stand for different messages: red = I love you; pink = I like you; white = friends; peppermint = secret admirer. A variation on this is to deliver the flowers but don't tell the recipient who they are from. If they want to know, they pay a specified amount to find out; senders can pay a higher fee to block the recipient from discovering their identity.

■ **Singing Telegrams.** Get together with your school chorus or recruit members of your organization who have good singing voices and sell singing telegrams to be delivered to classrooms on Valentine's Day or birthdays.

■ **Pizza by the Slice**. Local pizza places will often give schools a discount on pizza. If you have many students involved in after-school activities, sell slices of pizza in the time between the end of school and the start of activities and sports practices.

■ **Pie Sales.** Work with a local bakery to conduct a pie sale before Thanksgiving with a portion of the proceeds going to your group. Take orders for traditional pumpkin, pecan, and apple pies and deliver them the day before Thanksgiving.

■ **Breakfast Sales**. Sell fruit, donuts, bagels, yogurt, juice, and milk before school.

■ **T-shirt Sales**. Sell custom-designed shirts for special events at your school, such as a Homecoming shirt with this year's theme. Or, design a multipurpose spirit shirt that can be worn all year with each grade level having a designated color shirt and all shirts having the same design.

■ **Parking Space Sale.** Reserve the best student parking spots and sell them or auction them off at the beginning of each term.

■ **GST Auction**. Hold a Goods, Services, or Talents auction in which local businesses, parents, faculty members, and others donate items for an auction. Get a professional auctioneer to conduct it or do it as a silent auction.

Organizing a Successful Fundraiser

Start your fundraising effort by setting up a fundraising committee. This committee could be a standing committee that is charged with all fundraising efforts for the year, or it could be a special committee that works only on one particular fundraiser. Once you establish a committee, follow these steps to organize a successful fundraiser:

■ **Determine how much you need to raise.** Your group members should discuss why they want to raise money and how much they need. The goal you set will be a critical factor in determining the type of fundraiser needed. If your group needs to raise $3,000, you're not likely to choose a bake sale as your project. Once you know how much you need to raise, you can also determine how much each member of your group should have as a personal goal. Each person's individual goal is important to the success of the overall effort, since it's easier for each student to focus on a smaller, more achievable amount.

■ **Brainstorm ideas.** Brainstorming with the committee is a great way to start getting ideas for how to raise the money and gives everyone a chance to contribute. Remember to keep the group's goals in mind. Focus the brainstorming on things that could be done to help achieve overall goals.

■ **Make sure the activity is worth the effort.** Consider how much time and energy will be invested in the fundraiser and what the profit margin will be. There's no sense in putting in a huge effort for a small payoff.

■ **Attain group approval.** The committee should select the best fundraiser idea and present it to the entire organization at a meeting. Involve group members in a discussion of the proposal and vote on it. If all members of the group are going to be expected to participate, it's important that they all support the idea.

■ **Develop a plan.** Determine the steps involved in organizing the fundraiser you have selected. A product sale will involve different steps than a service or activity (see checklist on page 57). Refer to Chapter Two for guidance on project planning. Put your plan into action by having people sign up for the various subcommittees or tasks such as making posters, creating tickets, selling tickets, setting up and cleaning up, and so forth.

■ Get students excited about the project. The more you publicize your fundraiser, the more people will participate. Use attention-grabbing announcements, dynamic posters, fliers, bulletin boards, and other creative publicity techniques to draw attention to your efforts. (See page 32 for a publicity planning worksheet.)

■ Keep your goal in mind. Post your objective in a clearly visible spot and regularly update your progress. Help members see that their efforts are having the desired effect or, if the effort seems to be lagging, develop some incentives to motivate members to work harder. You might want to set aside a portion of the profits to establish individual and group incentives for reaching the goals. For a fundraiser in which products were sold, prizes for students who sell the most, for every student who reaches the goal, or for students who exceed the goal can help motivate students to higher sales levels.

■ Remember the details. Keep accurate records of inventory, individual sales, money turned in, and so forth. Thank everyone who helped in the effort—volunteers, parents, staff members, etc. Be sure to conduct an evaluation of the fundraiser when it is completed and file project report forms for future reference. (See Chapter Five.)

■ Celebrate your success! After the sales period or event is over, take time to celebrate your accomplishments. Remind yourselves what the money will be used for and congratulate yourselves on achieving your goals.

Student Organization Budget

Organization: _____

Adviser: _____ Year: _____

Planned Activities   **Anticipated Cost**

1. _____   _____

2. _____   _____

3. _____   _____

4. _____   _____

5. _____   _____

6. _____   _____

                          Subtotal: _____

Planned Fundraisers   **Anticipated Revenue**

1. _____   _____

2. _____   _____

3. _____   _____

4. _____   _____

5. _____   _____

6. _____   _____

                          Subtotal: _____

Anticipated Revenue – Anticipated Cost = Yearly Total: _____

Approval of Adviser:_____ Date: _____

Administrative Approval: _____ Date: _____

A Checklist for Fundraising

Here is a general checklist for product fundraising that can be customized for your particular needs and the requirements of your school district.

- ❏ Organize a fundraising steering committee.
- ❏ Review school policies and procedures for fundraising.
- ❏ Brainstorm possible fundraisers.
- ❏ List possible dates of fundraisers.
- ❏ Hold a group meeting to discuss proposed fundraisers and make final selection.
- ❏ Obtain approval of fundraiser by adviser, principal, school board, or other authority as determined by local policy.
- ❏ Select a vendor if applicable.
- ❏ Establish a timeline and schedule it on the master school calendar.
- ❏ Determine incentives.
- ❏ Sign contract with the vendor.
- ❏ Acknowledge parent and student responsibility.
- ❏ Hold sale kick-off event.
- ❏ Create and distribute individual student record sheets.
- ❏ Deposit money daily.
- ❏ Verify record sheets.
- ❏ Issue purchase order for sale inventory.
- ❏ Count and record initial inventory.
- ❏ Secure merchandise during delivery period.
- ❏ Secure and return unsold merchandise and complete final inventory.
- ❏ Conduct final reconciliation of the funds raised.
- ❏ Have final bill approved by students and adviser.
- ❏ Hold evaluation and recognition meeting.
- ❏ Write up final reports.
- ❏ Organize and file notes, records, and evaluations.
- ❏ Thank everyone who contributed to your success.

Chapter 5

EVALUATION

- -

IN THIS CHAPTER

▓ Reasons to Evaluate

▓ Steps in the Evaluation Process

▓ Evaluation Techniques

▓ Keeping Project Files

▓ Giving Constructive Feedback

▓ Evaluating School Traditions

- -

Evaluation is an important part of any student activities program. Many people think of evaluation as something to be done only at the end of a project or the end of the year, but if conducted properly, an evaluation can do much more than answer "what happened?" Used as an ongoing process, evaluation can help determine the strengths and weaknesses of a program or group and focus attention on needed improvements, even as the project or year is underway.

Reasons to Evaluate

No organization or activity can operate effectively without conducting some type of evaluation. It is easy to get caught up in planning and conducting activities and put off or give little formal attention to this phase of successful organization. But overlooking evaluation often means that groups continue to do things the same way, assuming that they are effective, rather than obtaining feedback that will aid in decision making and contribute to a stronger program. Some good reasons to evaluate include:

▓ **Cocurricular lessons**. Student activities are an important part of the educational mission of a school. Students learn many valuable lessons that will serve them throughout their lives. Taking the time to conduct an evaluation of each project or activity utilizes the teachable moments involved in each experience. What lessons were learned that could be applied to future experiences? How can student leaders grow from this experience?

▓ **Focus on goals.** Evaluation sessions enable group members to keep the focus on the goals they set for the year and for the project. How did this activity or project enable them to work toward or reach a goal?

■ **Continual improvement.** Analyzing weaknesses and discussing ways to improve them allows students to focus on continually improving their performance. Using the notes and reports from previous years' participants allows the group as a whole to grow and improve by capitalizing on the lessons learned from those who have gone before them. Adding their reports to the files

allows current members to contribute to the legacy of improvement.

■ **Celebrate achievement.** Pausing to evaluate the effectiveness of each project, meeting, or activity allows group members an opportunity to recognize each other's accomplishments and provide encouragement and support when needed.

Steps in the Evaluation Process

Whether you are conducting a quick, informal evaluation or one that is more elaborate and time consuming, evaluations generally follow the same steps:

1. Define the purpose of the evaluation.
Why are you conducting the evaluation? What do you want to be able to do with the information you gather? Is this for your group's use in planning the same project for next year? Do you want to determine how well group members work together? Will you present a report to the principal or school board to justify the continuation of the activity? The purpose of your evaluation will guide your decisions in the rest of the process.

2. Specify the scope of the evaluation.
Who should be involved in the evaluation? From what sources should information be collected? Planners? Participants? Observers? Others?

3. Determine the best way to collect data.
What method(s) will you use to gather information—questionnaires, interviews, focus groups, discussions, etc.?

Evaluation

To make evaluation successful it should:

E	Evolve around goals and objectives
V	Verify work of the organization and what others say is happening
A	Assist in self-evaluation by members
L	Lead to constructive suggestions
U	Utilize many techniques or devices
A	Result in Action based on feedback and data
T	Be Timely in assessing what is taking place
I	Involve many people
O	Be Objective and based upon data, not guesses
N	Notify others for program publicity and effectiveness.

Source: Earl Reum

4. Develop the evaluation method and data collection plan. Create your questionnaire, survey, list of questions, or other method. Determine how you will go about collecting the data. Set a date to complete data collection.

5. Collect the data. Hold your discussion, conduct the survey, talk to participants.

6. Analyze the data and prepare a report. Compile the information gathered in a report (see form on page 69) to share with group members, administration, and others who have an interest.

7. Use the evaluation report for program improvement. Keep the reports on file so they can be referred to by others who might be organizing a similar event in the future.

Evaluation Techniques

A number of techniques, both formal and informal, can be used to evaluate your projects and activities. Regardless of which technique you use, to be effective the evaluation should:

- Be administered in a short amount of time
- Be simple and uncomplicated
- Relate to group or project goals
- Involve people both inside and outside the organization—members, nonmembers, faculty, staff, administrators, parents, members of the community—depending on what is being evaluated
- Include data that is both objective—attendance figures, costs involved, number of hours expended, etc.—and subjective—

opinions about the project, thank you notes received, etc.

- Focus on actions, not people (what happened, not who is to blame)
- Record strengths and weaknesses
- Lead to constructive suggestions for the future.

With those characteristics in mind, select an evaluation technique that works best for your particular circumstances, and vary the techniques from project to project so members don't get into a stale routine when evaluating. Some possibilities include:

- **Random surveys**. Seek input from general members of the student body about events in which they were involved by conducting random surveys. Participants' perspectives often will be considerably different—sometimes positively, sometimes negatively—than those of group members who were involved in planning and organizing the event. When distributing surveys, take a random sample of students in different grade levels; also include faculty, staff, and administration. Distribute more surveys than you think you want, keeping in mind that not everyone will actually complete and return it. An alternative is to use one of the online survey tools such as Survey Monkey or Zoomerang and direct people to the survey's URL to complete it. This makes tallying responses easier, but means respondents must have access to a computer.

- **Interviews**. Armed with a set of standard questions relating to the event or program you are evaluating, send your members out

Creating an Effective Survey

Sometimes the best way to investigate and evaluate is by asking others. A survey or questionnaire might be just what you need. Here are some tips for creating an effective survey.

- **Purpose**: Why are you doing the survey? What do you want to know from or about your subjects? Make sure those objectives are related to your project.

- **Subjects**: Whom should you survey? Include only the people who can tell you what you need to know.

- **Unit and Sampling:** Decide what your unit of measure is. Are you looking at classrooms or individual students' attitudes? Changes in the entire school, or one particular group of students? Will you ask everyone, or just pick a sample? If you use a sample, find a way to be sure the sample group is similar to the entire student body (if that's what you're measuring).

- **Questions:** Write clear, simple questions. Stick to a single page and maybe 6–10 questions. Avoid negatives and essay-type questions. Use check-off choices and/or words that suggest a specific kind of answer.

- **Testing:** Try your questions out on a small group to make sure the questions are understood as you mean them to be. Make sure the answers give you useful information.

- **Method:** Decide whether you will mail the survey, distribute it during classes, use in-person teams for interviews, or ask questions by telephone or e-mail.

- **Execute the Survey:** Create a questionnaire, based on your tested questions, that allows appropriate space for answers to be filled in. Train interviewers, if needed, to ensure they will all discuss the survey the same way. Administer the survey to the group selected and collect the data.

- **Tabulate the Results:** Tally up the answers you get by type of answer. Don't forget to include a space to tally those who did not answer the question. Decide whether to count them or not. Once you decide, be consistent.

- **Analysis:** What's surprising? What's expected and what's not? Negative, positive, and divided responses (such as "no clear majority agreed on the need for ____") are important findings.

Excerpted from *Planning a Successful Crime Prevention Project,* Youth in Action, Washington, DC: U.S. Department of Justice, 1998.

to interview selected individuals. You might specify that each member must interview a student from each grade level in your school, a teacher, a parent, a support staff member, a community member, or some other person.

• **Questionnaires**. Create a questionnaire about the event or program with multiple choice answers that can be recorded on a bubble sheet for easy tabulation.

• **Group discussion**. Sometimes the best evaluation is just a discussion among group members. Some general questions to consider during the discussion include:

• What worked well?

• What didn't work very well?

• Did we achieve our goals?

• Was the result worth the effort?

• How was the workload? Did anyone carry too much of the load?

• Were all necessary supplies and materials obtained and in place?

• Were people involved given ample information?

• Did our plans adequately anticipate what would happen? Did anything unexpected occur?

• What can we learn from this experience for our next effort?

• **Bar graph evaluation**. On a blackboard or piece of flip-chart paper, create the format for a bar graph with numerical rankings along the bottom from 1 to 5. One corresponds to a poor ranking, and five equals an excellent or outstanding ranking, with the other numbers appropriately labeled fair, good, and great. Give sticky notes to everyone in the group and ask them to select a ranking from 1–5 and write comments on the note about the event, meeting, or activity that go along with their ranking. Ask them to post them on the graph in the column to which they belong. When all are finished, you'll have a nice visual representation of how the group thinks the project went, along with some written evaluative comments.

Keeping Project Files

An important step in the evaluation process is making use of all the information gathered and lessons learned. Effective student organizations keep files of the events they sponsor so they don't need to reinvent the wheel from year to year. It's a good idea to get into the practice of creating a file for each project and have committee chairs and officers contribute to it. Items that are in any way related to planning and carrying out the activity should be included, such as:

• A project timeline—when to do what

• Committee assignments and a breakdown of areas of responsibility for members

• Number of participants and total work-hours expended

• Copies of purchase orders and contracts

• Copies of correspondence, letters, memos

• Supply lists and sources

• Work order requests for custodial staff

• Sketches of set-up directions for tables, staging, etc.

- People involved and their contact information

- Samples of publicity, announcements, tickets, and programs

- Any communication with the faculty such as excused lists, special bell schedules, etc.

- Evaluation form that identifies problems encountered and recommendations for improvement. (See form on page 69.)

Any items that help provide an overview of the event or program should also be included, such as:

- Photos taken at the event to show decorations, set-up, etc.

- Copies of newspaper articles about the event

- Thank-you notes received

- Committee reports.

Develop an expectation that committee chairs will be responsible for compiling the files. After an event or activity, require the committee chairs and officers to complete a Project Evaluation form (see page 69) to add to the file along with any pertinent documentation.

The next time your organization sponsors that event—or one similar to it—the first thing the new committee chairs should do is get out the previous year's file and read it. New chairs don't have to do the project the same way—they should be encouraged to put their own creative stamp on it—but checking to see what has been done before allows them to avoid potential pitfalls and build on the successes of their predecessors.

If that particular activity hasn't been done before, checking files of similar projects can also provide guidance. In this way, each year's group of student leaders can capitalize on the experience of their predecessors.

Giving Constructive Feedback

What happens if you've evaluated a project or activity and found some elements of it to be lacking? Giving feedback to the student leaders involved in the project is essential to the growth and development of the student leader as well as the productivity of the organization. As an educator and activity adviser, you will sometimes need to work with the student leaders in your group to critique the work they are doing or their participation in the organization's activities. It's easy to provide positive feedback—people enjoy hearing that they've done a good job on a project or that you appreciate their hard work, and they respond favorably when you tell them. Some advisers are hesitant to give anything but positive feedback. They fear embarrassing the student or want to avoid an emotional reaction.

Keep in mind that constructive feedback is not criticism. While criticism is usually negative and judgmental, constructive feedback is positive and informative, giving specific details so the student can take action to improve. If given properly, feedback is usually appreciated—most people want to be competent, and giving them information that will help them to improve often motivates them to do so. Some tips for giving constructive feedback include:

■ **Identify the topic.** In the beginning of the conversation, make clear what you will be providing feedback about. Say something like, "I want to talk with you about the way you chaired the committee meeting," or "Can we chat about your responsibilities as publicity chair?"

■ **Share your intentions.** Before offering negative feedback, let the student know why you are doing so. Preface your remarks by saying something like, "My intention for talking with you about this is that I want our project to go smoothly so we can all be proud of the end result," or "I'm telling you this because I'm feeling very frustrated that the work is not getting done and it's important to me that this project is a success."

■ **Clarify expectations.** Go over expectations for the student's behavior and clarify what is expected on your part as the adviser. For example: "My understanding of the project is that you were going to…" or, "I expect members of this organization to attend all meetings unless they have spoken to me in advance to arrange an excused absence."

■ **Focus on behavior.** Instead of making generalizations about the person, provide specific examples of behavior that needs to be adjusted or describe objective consequences that have or will occur. Vague criticism fosters anxiety. If you don't have specific examples, don't provide the feedback. Use I-messages to make your key points, such as "I have noticed…" or "I have seen…."

■ **Ask questions.** Guide the student to a better understanding of his or her behavior and others' perceptions of it by asking questions. This can also help you better understand how the student understood his or her role and what was expected. For example, "What was your response when…" or "How do you think you could have handled that better?"

■ **Remember the positive.** Don't focus only on negative behavior or things that need to be improved. Search for something positive to comment on as well, even if it's only the student's willingness to talk with you and listen to your suggestions. One good practice is to make a list of at least five things you appreciate about the student and his or her contributions to the organization before you begin a feedback session. Share some of these things with the student to help establish a positive rapport.

■ **Be careful not to mix your message** by saying something like "Taylor, you have worked hard on this project *but*…." This creates a contradiction and is likely to make the recipient disregard the first part of the message. Putting "but" in the middle—what some people think of as an acronym for "Behold the Unvarnished Truth"—basically tells the other person to not believe anything said before.

■ **Make it timely.** Feedback is best given soon after the behavior. Don't wait until the end of the quarter or semester to let a student know what he or she needs to improve. Seize the teachable moment, while an activity is fresh in the student's mind, to provide feedback about it. This also helps avoid the problem of overloading the student with feedback. Providing too many suggestions for change reduces the possibility that the student will be able to act on any of it; he or she may feel overwhelmed.

■ **Watch your tone.** Especially in a negative feedback situation, be careful of your tone of voice and body language. A concerned tone helps the student be receptive to your feedback and helps him or her understand your role as an educator in trying to foster improvement. Anger, frustration, disappointment, and sarcasm can turn the message into criticism and make the student less willing to hear what you have to say. The purpose of negative feedback should be to help the student strengthen his or her skills as a leader and a member of your organization. If you can't give negative feedback in a helpful manner, you defeat its purpose.

■ **Focus on improving.** Present the feedback as a method of strengthening student leadership and develop specific steps the student can take to improve his or her performance. Ask, "Next time you're in a similar situation, what will you do to handle it better?"

■ **Set a timeline.** After discussing the steps the student can take to improve, determine an appropriate time to get together to discuss the student's progress.

■ **Verify understanding.** No matter how positive your intentions are, any sort of constructive criticism is often threatening and may be misinterpreted. Check the student's understanding of the feedback by asking him or her to summarize the main points of the discussion. Re-emphasize any points that don't seem to have sunk in or clarify misperceptions.

■ **End on a positive note.** Finish the discussion with some positive, motivating comments that help the student understand that you value his or her contributions to your organization and find him or her to be a worthwhile member.

Evaluating School Traditions

In addition to evaluating the individual projects your organization sponsors, it's valuable to look periodically at your activities program as a whole to consider what school traditions have become outdated.

Barriers to Effective Feedback

Many factors can get in the way of effective feedback. Be careful to avoid these in your feedback session:

- Faulty assumptions
- Distorted perceptions
- Defensiveness
- Misreading body language
- Ignoring nonverbal cues
- Selective hearing
- Misunderstood language
- Failing to be candid
- Lack of sincerity
- Power struggles

Sometimes events on the school calendar are time-honored customs that have been carefully cultivated as important elements of the school year, and sometimes they spring up because, as every activity adviser knows, if you do something two years in a row it must be a tradition.

Often traditions are associated with big events on the school calendar like Homecoming, prom, and graduation. But sometimes a well-loved activity that a group sponsors each year becomes a tradition that students look forward to just as much as the bigger events—the food drive competition, a male beauty pageant, a talent show. Busy activity advisers often find themselves with a calendar that just keeps growing every year, as student leaders come up with new activities to add. Somehow, nothing ever seems to be subtracted because it's a "tradition."

If you find yourself in this position, it's time to evaluate the traditions your group is responsible for and decide if they are worth keeping. Consider the following points as you evaluate what is worthy of keeping and what can be eliminated or adjusted.

■ **Conduct a month-by-month review** of all the activities your group sponsors. Are they concentrated around a particular event or season? Perhaps your group goes all out for holiday activities or plans several events around graduation. Like a juggler with too many balls in the air, the more activities you have going on at once the higher your stress level is bound to be. Is there a way some of these activities can be moved to slower times

of the year? For example, a food drive is traditional at Thanksgiving, but food banks also need food at other times of the year. How about holding a "stock up for summer" food drive in the spring? Look for lulls in the calendar and see if any events can be shifted to the slower times.

■ **Consider the vitality of the tradition.** Look at the number of people who participate in the activity and their level of interest for doing so. If participation is lackluster, perhaps the tradition has run its course. Would anyone miss it if it stopped happening? Also consider how excited the members of your group are to work on making the activity happen. If they aren't eager to work on it, that could be a sign that the student body won't be eager to participate in it either.

■ **Identify the purpose of the tradition.** What function does the tradition serve? Is it designed to build class unity? To showcase school spirit? To raise money? Getting at the main reason for having the activity can help identify ways to improve or eliminate it. For example, if having each class create a banner for Homecoming to display at the game is designed to allow artistic students to participate in Homecoming activities, take a look at who actually works on the banners. Is it the same ol' people who do everything else? Is it one more burden for the class officers to carry at a time when they are already overloaded? If so, what can be done to involve the people the activity is intended to involve? Perhaps the art club could take over this aspect of Homecoming. By considering what the purpose of the tradition is, groups can decide whether it's time to either let this tradition go or plan a new one that serves the same purpose.

Consider how the activity supports the goals of your group. Ask yourselves "why do we do this?" and "why is it important?" If the activity no longer relates to one of your group's goals, why continue to sponsor it? If it does still have relevance, consider what elements of the event are worth keeping and plan ways to revitalize the activity.

Consider how long-standing the tradition is. If a particular tradition dates back to the founding of the school, maybe it's worth keeping just for that reason. If so, do a bit of research in old yearbooks and newspaper archives and publicize the rich history of the tradition. Develop school pride in the long-standing nature of the activity and help students and others see that they are part of something bigger than their particular year.

Evaluate whether the tradition supports school goals. Meet with the administration to talk about whether the traditions are helping or hindering the overall school goals. Are the activities helping to promote a positive school climate? Helping to engage students and develop a connection to the school? Supporting the academic mission? If a tradition isn't adding value to the school's mission, it should be discontinued.

Making a Change

Some activities can be modified or eliminated and no one will mind much. A few comments like, "it didn't used to be like this, did it?" will be made, but school life will go on pretty much the same. There are other events that are so ingrained in the life of the school or community that changing them can cause many repercussions—canceling a Homecoming parade, eliminating the Sadie Hawkins dance, or changing the way elections are held, for example.

If your group decides to change an activity it has sponsored that is considered an ingrained tradition, proceed carefully. Develop a plan for making the change and be sure to involve others—students, teachers, principals, parents—in the process. Remember the adage that people support what they help to create. The more people there are who can feel that they have a hand in developing something, the more people will support it.

Plan also to develop a public relations plan for publicizing the change; let people know the rationale for the change, what the new way entails, how the new method of doing things will be better. Use morning announcements, the school newspaper, the principal's newsletter, e-mails, even press releases to the local paper if it's something that involves the community. Get the word out so people will understand the change and more people will be likely to support it.

Then just be prepared to weather the storm. Not everyone will like the change and some will complain. But keep in mind that in a year or two, the new way will become the tradition, and people won't want to change it either!

Project Evaluation

Project Title: _____

Date(s) of Project: _____

Brief Description of Project: _____

How would you rate the success of this project?　❏ Outstanding　❏ Good　❏ Needs Improvement

What goals did the project achieve? _____

How many people are needed to do the work to organize this project?　　_____

How many people attended or participated in this project?　　_____

Attach a sheet listing the income from this project.　　Total income: _____

Attach a sheet listing the expenses incurred for this project.　　Total expenses: _____

Subtract expenses from income to calculate profit: _____

When should planning begin? How much time is needed to prepare and carry out this project? Briefly indicate a timeline for planning this project. Attach additional sheets, if needed.

One month before:

Two weeks before:

One week before:

Two days before:

One day before:

Day of event:

What problems did you encounter in planning this project and how were they resolved?

List the aspects of the project that you would do again:

Describe the aspects of the project that should be changed or improved next time it is held:

Other comments or suggestions for future chairs of this event:

Attach a list of all people, businesses, or groups who need thank-you notes.

Project ❏ Should ❏ Should Not be on next year's calendar. Why?

Attach additional information such as supply orders, work requests for custodians, receipts, programs, planning sheets, worker duties, announcement requests, and so forth that may be helpful to the next chairperson of this project.

Evaluation completed by: _____

Chapter 6

RECOGNITION

"Thank you!"

"You really did a nice job with that."

"I appreciate your efforts!"

It doesn't take much to let someone know their efforts have been noticed and appreciated. Yet how many people go through each day never receiving positive feedback for the things they do? As a student activity adviser, it's easy to get swept up in the hectic pace of juggling teaching responsibilities and personal obligations while jumping from one activity to another. You appreciate the contributions of student leaders, volunteers, faculty members, and parents, but how often do you take the time to let them know how much you value their efforts?

A logical step after evaluating a project or program (see Chapter Five) is to recognize the contributions and achievements of those who took part in it. Just as evaluation is a continuous process, recognition should take place on an ongoing basis. If you wait until the end of the year to recognize members and volunteers, you will find yourself with a diminished group of people to recognize!

Reasons for Recognition

Recognizing contributions is important for several reasons:

▓ **Keep up morale.** Student leaders and others often work long, hard hours to develop and pull off an activity or program, and usually to not much fanfare. Participants in the activity rarely give much thought to how it came to happen, they just enjoy it. It's not likely that your student leaders will be deluged with compliments on how well they organized an event or chaired a meeting. Continually working hard without having your efforts recognized can be very discouraging. Students may begin wondering "what's the point of working hard? No one notices anyway." Taking the time to acknowledge contributions of your student leaders will go a long way toward keeping their spirits up.

■ **Develop camaraderie.** Building a culture of recognition promotes a supportive, positive environment where people enjoy both what they do and those with whom they do it. This will also help in your efforts to recruit new members from year to year.

■ **Have fun.** Recognition doesn't have to be formal to be effective. Humorous "awards" handed out during your evaluation session after a big project serve multiple purposes: you'll recognize contributions, release tensions, and have some fun at the same time.

■ **Encourage exemplary behavior.** If there's an area in which members could use some improvement—let's say they're having trouble making it to meetings on time—start rewarding the behavior you want to see and watch how quickly it improves. For example, give every person who comes on time to the next meeting a mini candy bar or other treat. Students who see others being recognized for their hard work, positive attitudes, and team spirit will be encouraged to adopt these behaviors themselves.

■ **Encourage further contributions.** On a practical note, if you expect to ever have people help you again, it would be wise

to recognize them for their contributions. Everyone likes to feel appreciated and no one likes to be taken for granted. Those who receive recognition are encouraged to continue helping and are likely to help even more next time their help is needed.

Recognition Takes Many Forms

Because different people are motivated by different forms of acknowledgment, your recognition program should be diversified. A one-size-fits-all effort of giving all your volunteers a certificate of recognition isn't likely to generate a feeling of true appreciation.

To be meaningful, recognition must be personalized. Mass-produced thank-you notes that all say the same thing are likely to be tossed in the trash and leave their recipients feeling disgruntled. "I did all that and all they sent me was a lousy photocopied note!" Tailoring your recognition to the personality and motivation of individuals takes extra time, but is well worth the effort in the long run.

When developing your recognition program, consider some of the following ideas.

Member Recognition

• **Thank-you notes.** Never underestimate the value of a hand-written note, especially one that singles out a particular element that's pertinent to the recipient. Be specific in mentioning the recipient's contribution to the project: "chairing the back to school bash," "organizing the faculty appreciation lunch," and so forth. Notice the little things your group members do—"staying late to help with the clean-up," "being the first to volunteer"—to contribute to the success of an event and comment on it in your notes.

- **Notes with trinkets.** Create a special sheet of notepaper or a notecard with a design that's relevant to the project and write the notes immediately after its conclusion. For example, on the Monday following Homecoming Week, you might send a notecard or notepaper that says, "Thanks for your help raisin' school spirit" along with a small box of raisins (chocolate covered?) and a hand-written message detailing the recipient's contributions to the success of the week. (See "Ideas for Trinkets" on page 74.)

- **Public Praise.** Acknowledge members' contributions at meetings by calling them up to the front of the meeting room and telling everyone what a good job they did. Allow other members to chime in with their thoughts and appreciations as well.

- **Sticker Splash.** Give every member of your group a blank sheet of address labels or other stickers and ask them to write compliments and thank-you comments to all the other members of your group. At your evaluation meeting, have members walk around and stick the labels on each other.

- **Humorous awards**. Give individualized certificates—easily created on the computer—to each member of the group at the completion of a big project. Examples of this type of creative and meaningful awards

include "Cinderella" for always doing the dirty work, "Super Saver" attached to a roll of Lifesavers for the individual who saved the project, "Night Owl" for putting in extra long hours, "Hakuna Matata" for always having a positive outlook, and "Ever-Ready" for the person who was always there to help.

- **Locker signs**. Take your member recognition into the school by creating attractive individualized locker signs to recognize contributions. Tape the signs on members' lockers before school one day. Add balloons and streamers for some extra attention.

- **Bulletin board.** Create a bulletin board with the names and photos of chairpeople for a big project with some text identifying what they did and thanking them for a job well done.

- **Key chains.** Find appropriate key chains to give as recognition, such as a steering wheel keychain for the members of a steering committee, a key to signify a member being "the key to our success," or a globe to let them know they made a "world of difference."

- **Letter to parents.** Send a letter to your students' parents praising their efforts and accomplishments and thanking the parents for their support. Be specific!

- **End of year letter.** Draft a letter to the faculty at the end of the year that describes the accomplishments of your group members and invites the faculty and staff members to join you in congratulating

Ideas for Trinkets and Thoughts

Many small items available at craft stores, discount stores, candy stores, or carnival supply stores can be used in clever ways to express appreciation in thank-you notes. Next time you need to say "thank you," try the following:

- Jeweled star on the end of a two-inch pipe cleaner or toothpick to make a "magic wand" with "Thanks for the magic you made happen for…"
- A die with "No matter how you roll the dice, your hard work on the ___ paid off!"
- Birthday cake candle with "Although it seemed you had to burn the candle at both ends, your hard work made the ___ a flaming success!"
- Bundle of miniature silk roses with "You certainly deserve a dozen roses for your hard work on our ___."
- Faceted "jewels" with "You've been a jewel to work so hard to make the ___ successful."
- Fish stickers or erasers with "I know you're not fishing for compliments, but your work as ___ was an outstanding success," or "I know it seemed as if you were sometimes swimming upstream, but your hard work on the ___ project certainly paid off."
- Globe key chain with "Your help on the ___ was worth the world," or "There's no one on earth like you! The ___ wouldn't have happened without your hard work."
- Paper clip chain with "Your hard work on the ___ held our group together!"
- Wrapped peppermint candy with "The work you put in on the ___ was worth a mint! Thank you so much for your help!"
- Piece of chalk with "Chalk up another successful ___! Thanks for ___ to ensure its accomplishment!"
- Hand or mitten-shaped mini cookie cutter or wooden cutout with "Thanks for lending a hand at the ___. Your help made it the success it was!"
- Stick of gum with "You really stuck to it in order to make the ___ successful!"
- Crayon with "You made your mark on ___. You can color it completely successful."
- A key (blanks or buy a bunch of old ones at an auction or flea market) with "Your hard work on the ___ was the key to its success!"
- Plastic star-shaped bead with "Thanks for being the star of the ___."
- Candy bars (miniature ones are cheaper) can be accompanied by a variety of corresponding messages. For example, "An extra Payday (or $100,000) is the least you deserve for your hard work on ___." Or, "When it came down to Crunch time, your help on the ___ made all the difference in doing a great job!" Or, "I just have Mounds of praise for your hard work on the ___ project."

Excerpted from "Muchas Gracias: The ABCs of Saying Thanks," by Barb Lord in the April 1998 issue of *Leadership for Student Activities*.

your student leaders on a job well done. List each project and its chair so faculty can make specific comments.

Faculty and Staff Recognition

Another important group to recognize for its support is the faculty and staff. Try these ideas:

- **Singing telegram.** Express appreciation for the assistance of the school secretaries by having your group members join together to serenade them or deliver a singing telegram.

- **Letter to the principal.** Send a letter of commendation to the principal detailing the way a faculty or staff member went out of his or her way to assist with an activity. Be sure to cc: the staff member.

- **Extra payday.** Give teachers who chaperone an activity a Payday candy bar with a note that reads: "We wish we could give you an extra payday for your help."

- **Faculty raffle**. Conduct a monthly drawing at faculty meetings for prizes that your group purchases or has donated from local businesses. Give every teacher a ticket, but present extra tickets just before the drawing to those who have helped in some way and be sure to publicly announce why they are receiving the extra tickets.

- **Posters**. Make a poster expressing your appreciation for a faculty or staff member's help, have all your group members sign it, and hang it on the door of the person's classroom or office. Or, create a large banner for a group of faculty or staff members who helped with something and hang it where they can see it. For example, hang a poster on the wall across from the cafeteria kitchen stating "We Love Our Cafeteria Staff!" in recognition of their assistance with a faculty appreciation breakfast.

- **Bulletin announcements.** Recognize the efforts of individuals or groups in bulletin announcements and encourage students and staff members to thank them also.

- **Bobblehead Banner.** Create a thank-you banner for the office staff by taking enlarged photos of your members' heads and attaching them to a stick figure body on a butcher paper banner. Draw talk balloons coming from each person with a positive recollection of an interaction they had with the office or a reason they appreciate the staff.

- **Assembly recognition.** Bring out the custodians or cafeteria staff at an assembly and ask the students to show their appreciation for all their hard work.

Community and Parent Volunteer Recognition

Don't forget to recognize parents and community members who support your program.

- **Thank-you notes.** Be sure to write a letter to all the people and businesses that donated time or materials to any project. Specifically identify what the recipient did and how it contributed to your success. Include the value of any items donated and the school's federal tax ID number so the letter can be used as a tax receipt. Deliver the letters in person if possible and verbally express your appreciation as well.

- **Newsletter items.** Write an item for the school's newsletter thanking businesses and individuals who have donated time, money, services, or products.

- **Newspaper ad.** Take out an ad in the local paper identifying volunteers and businesses who have helped. Thank them for their contributions and encourage community members to support them.

- **Letter to the editor.** Write a letter to the editor of the local paper expressing your appreciation for the community's support of a particular activity or program. Be sure to mention, by name, specific individuals who have been instrumental in the program's success.

- **Grand marshal.** Select a community member who has been especially supportive and designate him or her as the Grand Marshal of your Homecoming parade.

- **Volunteer of the Year.** Recognize a person who has helped throughout the year with a volunteer of the year award at your end-of-year banquet or other recognition activity.

APPENDIX 1
National Student Leadership Organizations

DECA
1908 Association Dr.
Reston, VA 20191
703-860-5000
www.deca.org
DECA prepares emerging leaders and entrepreneurs in marketing, finance, hospitality and management in high schools and colleges around the globe.

Family, Career and Community Leaders of America (FCCLA)
1910 Association Dr.
Reston, VA 20191
703-476-4900
www.fcclainc.org
High school chapters promote personal growth and leadership development in young men and women through family and consumer sciences education.

Future Business Leaders of America (FBLA)
1912 Association Dr.
Reston, VA 20191
703-860-3334
www.fbla.org
This organization is open to high school and college students preparing for business or office careers.

Health Occupations Students of America (HOSA)
6021 Morris Rd., Suite 111
Flower Mound, TX 75028
800-321-HOSA
www.hosa.org
A vocational student organization whose mission is to enhance the delivery of compassionate, quality health care and promote career opportunities in the health care industry.

Key Club International
3636 Woodview Trace
Indianapolis, IN 46268-3196
317-875-8755, ext. 273
www.keyclub.org
High school service organization sponsored by local Kiwanis Clubs.

National 4-H Council
7100 Connecticut Ave.
Chevy Chase, MD 20815-4999
301-961-2800
www.4-h.org

The mission of the National 4-H Council is to build partnerships for community youth development that value and involve youth in solving issues critical to their lives, their families, and society.

National Association of Student Councils

1904 Association Dr.
Reston, VA 20191
703-860-0200
www.nasc.us

Representing middle level and high school councils nationwide, NASC aims to help all student councils become more effective organizations by focusing on training students to become effective leaders.

National FFA Organization

P.O. Box 68960
6060 FFA Drive
Indianapolis, IN 46268-0960
Phone: 317-802-6060
www.ffa.org

Develops student potential for leadership, personal growth, and career success through agricultural education.

National Honor Society
National Junior Honor Society

1904 Association Dr.
Reston, VA 20191
703-860-0200
www.nhs.us and *www.njhs.us*

The nation's premier organizations established to recognize outstanding middle level and high school students who have demonstrated excellence in scholarship, leadership,

service, and character (and citizenship for NJHS).

Skills USA

14001 James Monroe Hwy.
P.O. Box 3000
Leesburg, VA 20175
703-777-8810
www.skillsusa.org

For high school and college students interested in technical, skilled, and service occupations.

Technology Student Association (TSA)

1914 Association Dr.
Reston, VA 20191-1540
703-860-9000
www.tsaweb.org

Devoted to the needs of elementary, middle, and high school students with a dedicated interest in technology.

APPENDIX 2
Professional Development for Advisers

Most adviser training occurs on the job, after an educator has accepted the responsibility for guiding a student activity. While sometimes difficult to find, opportunities for professional development in student activity advising exist at the state and national levels.

■ **State associations.** Many state education associations offer training for advisers through weekend or summer workshops. Check with your state principals' association, your state student council association, the state interscholastic activities association, the state adviser for our cocurricular activity, or the state department of education.

■ **Alliance for Student Activities.** Founded by a group of educators and trainers who realized the need for a unifying voice and network to promote the benefits and processes of cocurricular activities, the Alliance focuses on training, resources, networking and advocacy. Professional Development Academies are one-day training opportunities for advisers offered at various locations, while Adviser Seminars are weekend training opportunities. Visit *www.alliance4studentactivities.org* for more information.

■ **CADA Conference.** The California Association of Directors of Activities' annual conference is an excellent place to attend workshops, hear speakers, and network with other advisers. CADA welcomes advisers from other states who want to attend, and has even created a "regional" group (Area H) for folks who are not from California. The conference is typically held in late February or early March and is well worth attending. For information, visit *www.cada1.org*.

■ **LEAD Conferences.** The National Association of Student Councils, the National Honor Society, and the National Junior Honor Society join forces to sponsor three weekend conferences for student leaders and their advisers in various parts of the country each spring. Workshops are presented by veteran advisers and student leaders, and there are a variety of keynote speakers and presentations by national office staff members. Visit *www.nasc.us* or *www.nhs.us* for more information.

■ **STAR Leaders Conference.** The STAR Leaders National Student Conference brings together adviser and student delegates from

NHS, NJHS, and the National Association of Student Councils for three days focused on enhancing their leadership abilities and improving their chapter and council programs. Visit *www.nhs.us* or *www.nasc.us* for more information.

■ **National Conference on Student Activities.** For 30 years the National Association of Workshop Directors (NAWD)—a professional organization for activity advisers and workshop directors founded by Dr. Earl Reum—has been sponsoring a national conference where members meet and share information focusing on leadership development and student activities. The conference is held the first weekend in December and rotates to a different part of the country each year. This adviser-only conference features speakers and a wide variety of workshops. Veteran attendees count it as one of the highlights of their year. For more information visit *www.nawd.com* or e-mail *nawdoffice@aol.com*.

■ **National associations.** Check with the national association affiliated with the area of student activities you are advising such as FCCLA for family and consumer sciences, DECA for marketing, National Honor Society, Key Club, and so forth. Most of these organizations offer national conferences and many offer regional or state workshops as well. (See Appendix 1 for a listing of these organizations.)

APPENDIX 3

Resources

The Internet is a mind-boggling collection of resources on any topic imaginable, and student activities is no exception. Intrepid searchers can find a wealth of resources, ideas, and supplies for their student leadership activities.

In the course of my work as an editor for various student activity publications, I am constantly coming across new resources. With the ever-shifting nature of the Internet, providing a static list of recommended sites in this publication (as the first edition of this book did) would not be the most helpful resource for advisers. I do keep a current list of websites I find worthwhile on my website at *http://www.leadershiplogistics.us/resources/* and I use Delicious social bookmarking as well. I find the Delicious bookmarks particularly helpful because the tool allows you to tag a website with key-words for easy retrieval later. For example, by visiting my bookmarks at *http://www.delicious.com/LynFiscus* you can see all the sites I have tagged with "fundraising" or "dances" or "productivity." If you are looking for good resources on a particular topic related to student activities, I recommend you access my Delicious bookmarks for a current list of websites I find useful or relevant. Look on the right side of the page for a list of tags I use.

Suggested Reading

Similarly, there is a wealth of publications available for those who are interested in furthering their knowledge of leadership development and student activities. Rather than provide a static list here, I refer you to the recommended reading list I keep on the Leadership Teacher website at *http://leadershipteacher.webnode.com/recommended-reading/*. The books are listed by such categories as meeting skills, project planning, citizenship, leadership, and so forth.

ABOUT THE AUTHOR

Lyn Fiscus has been active in the field of student activities for nearly three decades. Her involvement has evolved from active advising to publishing and presenting about student activities.

Lyn taught at the high school level in the St. Louis area for 12 years—10 of those years as a leadership class teacher—and worked with a variety of student groups including student council, yearbook, newspaper, SADD, TREND, pep club, cheerleaders, and American Youth Foundation (AYF) Leadership Compact. She served as assistant director of the Missouri Association of Student Councils (MASC) summer leadership workshop, represented the St. Louis area on the MASC Executive Board for six years, and served on staff of NASSP's National Leadership Camps, becoming co-director of the NLC in New York. In addition, she served as a staff member of AYF's International Leadership Camp for four years, is a former executive board member of the National Association of Student Activity Advisers, and is a frequent presenter at student activities conferences. She was instrumental in the founding of the Alliance for Student Activities, a nonprofit association to promote the value of student activities, and she serves as its vice president.

Lyn was the editor of the award-winning *Leadership for Student Activities*, published by NASSP for student council and National Honor Society advisers, from 1995–2007. She also served as editor of DECA's *Dimensions* magazine from 2006 to 2009, and was editorial consultant for FCCLA's *Teen Times* magazine from 2005 to 2010. She has worked with the Technology Student Association (TSA), SkillsUSA, Herff Jones, Inc., National Middle School Association (NMSA), the National Association of Workshop Directors (NAWD), the California Association of Directors of Activities (CADA), National Organizations for Youth Safety (NOYS), and state student council organizations in Texas, Pennsylvania, Oregon, Michigan, Indiana, and Wisconsin. She currently manages Leadership Logistics, a company she founded in 2004, which provides writing, editing, training, and publishing services to support positive youth development.

Lyn is the author of *Adviser Essentials: Project Planning* (2010) and *Who Says You Can't Change the World* (1991). She served as editor/writer of the *National Leadership Camp Leadership Curriculum Guide* (1994) and TASSP's *Student Leadership* course curriculum guide (2008). She is co-author of *The Bucks Start Here: Fundraising for Student Activities* (2007) with Earl Reum, and is the founder of the *Leadership Teacher* website.

In 2005, she was the national recipient of the Earl Reum Award, given by the National Association of Workshop Directors (NAWD) in recognition of outstanding leadership and commitment to the promotion of excellence in student activities. She lives in Reston, Virginia, with her husband and two children.

Also Available from Leadership Logistics

Adviser Essentials: Project Planning by Lyn Fiscus offers guidance for both novice and veteran advisers on how to help student leaders work through some of the usual tasks that are common to all projects and encourage them to consider aspects they might not think of on their own. By making the use of the information and forms in *Adviser Essentials: Project Planning* part of your project planning routine, student leaders will begin to develop their own expertise at project planning. (45 pages) $8.95 plus S/H

The Bucks $tart Here: Fundraising for Student Activities, by Lyn Fiscus and Earl Reum, offers hundreds of ideas for fundraising projects and sales that will put the fun back in fundraising. Try activities like an airband contest, dancing with the staff show, duct-taping the principal to a wall, or teacher dares that will involve lots of students, create excitement and positive school spirit, and bring in much-needed money for your treasury. This essential resource for anyone who conducts school fundraisers also features:

- Project planning guides for organizing fundraisers
- Tips for selecting and working with vendors
- Ideas for making money through group activities
- Budgeting for events and organizations
- Pitfalls to avoid
- Fundraising resources
- Reproducible forms
- And much more!

(64 pages) $14.95 plus S/H

DVD Toolbox Series: Effective FUNdraising Learn how to plan, execute, and process fundraising activities to maximize their cocurricular compoents by providing an opportunity for many people to be involved in something significant. This class discusses the essential elements of an effective fundraising compaign and prvides a wealth of creative fundraising ideas. Based on the book, *The Bucks $tart Here: Fundraising for Student Activities*, by Lyn Fiscus and Earl Reum. Program includes one 38-minute DVD video that includes printable support/resource materials on the disc. $42.00 plus S/H

To order visit *www.leadershiplogistics.us*

Made in the USA
Lexington, KY
02 June 2017